"I LE PARADE!"

Main Street Memories

Bev —
Your Paul,
Dean

"I LED THE PARADE!"
Main Street Memories

DEAN GASCHLER

Another Quality Book Published By:
LEGACY BOOK PUBLISHING
1883 Lee Road, Winter Park, FL 32789
WWW.LEGACYBOOKPUBLISHING.com

"I Led the Parade": Main Street Memories

Published by:
LEGACY Book Publishing
1883 Lee Road
Winter Park, Florida 32789
www.LegacyBookPublishing.com

© Dean Gaschler 2013
Printed in the United States
ISBN: 978-1-937952-45-7

Cover Design by Gabriel H. Vaughn
Original Cover artwork by Gabriel Molano

DEDICATION

To Linda,
my wife and closest friend.
Love always

Foreword

By Lee Cockerell

It turns out that I had the second best role in the show at Walt Disney World. I was in charge of making sure each of our 65,000 cast members were creating magic for millions of guests from around the world day in and day out.

Dean Gaschler, on the other hand, had the very best role as he actually made sure the magic happened. Dean held the unique and important role of Grand Marshal Coordinator for the Magic Kingdom, a position he held for 14 of the 21 years he created magic for Disney guests.

Dean was privileged to select the family (or families) to be in the three o'clock parade every day. He was responsible for planning and escorting these special guests, including my family and me, on the occasion of my retirement. And, most important, he had the privilege of selecting the Veteran of the Day to participate in the Magic Kingdom Flag Retreat...our Stars and Stripes at the end of each day.

These events are the most emotional, exciting, and memorable parts of the day for all Disney World guests and for Disney cast members. I assure you that millions have shed tears at these events through the years.

Dean's magical book, *"I Led the Parade: Main Street Memories"*, will give all Disney fans a glimpse of a special part of the magic that is only known to Dean himself. If you love Disney World, you will love this book! As I read it I too found out all of the special moments I missed through the years. Dean has captured those moments for all of us to enjoy.

—Lee Cockerell
Exec. Vice President Walt Disney World Resort
(Retired and Inspired)

Lee Cockerell is also the author of two books; *Creating Magic: 10 Common Sense Leadership Strategies from a Life at Disney* and *The Customer Rules: The 39 Essential Rules for Delivering Sensational Service*

Acknowledgements

Where to begin? So very many to thank. I'll start with the entire cast at Walt Disney World, particularly the Magic Kingdom. The park is always beautiful and "show ready" for the cast and guests.

I was honored to be a part of both the Magic Kingdom Cosmetology and Guest Relations Cast. Additionally, I worked closely with the Entertainment Department. Thank you, Dapper Dans, Streetmosphere, Parade Management, and countless characters and performers.

There's literally hundreds of cast members that deserve to be mentioned. I'm sorry that space does not allow; please know how important you are to me.

A few individuals **must** be mentioned: Dave Krazit and Marvin Smith, leaders extraordinaire! Jim Vais, an amazing friend. Angela Bowles and Jodi White...nothing was ever "out of the question" for you. Those literally "hands on" deserve special thanks. Lee Cockerell, Michael Thomas MacGillivray, and Rebekah Lyn...without you, this would not have happened.

And most of all, I want to thank God...without Him, **nothing** happens.

INTRODUCTION

Each day in the Magic Kingdom thousands of guests observe the immensely popular three o'clock parade. Some line up nearly an hour in advance in an attempt to locate the perfect spot. The parade route is always packed.

Lucky families are selected to participate as that day's Honorary Grand Marshals. Have you ever wondered how this happens? For fourteen years of my career at Walt Disney World it was my responsibility to select these individuals. This book will share stories from some of the nearly 7,000 parties I selected.

In 1991, I began my duties with Disney in the Harmony Barber Shop, located on Main Street USA. After seven years, I applied for and was awarded the Grand Marshal Coordinator position. The gentleman that had selected the Grand Marshals for over eight years was retiring due to health issues.

The parade's name changed many times over the years. The name was themed with the specific "celebration" at the time. Examples include *Share A Dream Come True Parade, Magical Moments Parade, and 100 Years Of Magic Parade*. It was always exciting to witness the creativity that went into each new presentation.

So what did I look for in the families I would select? The guests needed to be happy and outgoing. Their plans would have to include the Magic Kingdom for the day. Party size was a factor as well; the parade vehicle could not accommodate a large family reunion.

The rest was instinct and experience. In my role as a greeter, I would approach prospective guests asking if they needed assistance or directions. And, yes, guests would sometimes approach me. My interview questions were generic, discreet, and open-ended. Then, I would listen and observe. Guests would often talk themselves into (or out of) being asked to be Grand Marshals. Each day was unique, one of the things I loved about the position.

Once I made my selection, I'd gather the names and hometowns of the special guests. This was announced along the parade route and was one of the highlights for the Grand Marshals... (Ladies and Gentlemen, Boys and Girls, please welcome the Smith Family from Dallas, Texas). They were also presented with personalized Mickey Mouse "ear" hats and certificates proclaiming their parade participation. For many, it was indeed their "fifteen minutes of fame."

In addition, during my last year with Disney I selected the Honorary Veteran of the Day for the Flag Retreat Ceremony. Several chapters of this book are stories regarding our Veterans.

About ninety-nine percent of my Marshals were day guests who were selected on a random basis. On occasion, I would host celebrities. These 'high profile' people would normally be selected weeks in advance and many times would be associated with a special event the park was hosting or sponsoring. This was the case on my very first day as Grand Marshal Coordinator. On to Chapter One to meet this very special lady!

From 1991 - 1998 Dean made magic for Guests at the
Harmony Barber Shop, Main Street USA

Mainstreet Memory I

No First Day Jitters

I began my 14-year stint as Grand Marshal Coordinator in April, 1998, a brand new role in a brand new department for me. A high-profile individual had been selected on my first day. My new manager felt this would be good experience for me. In my new position, I would be dealing with celebrities on a routine basis.

Our special guest was the (then) Treasurer of The United States, Mary Ellen Withrow. What an introduction to my new career! She was a very pleasant and outgoing lady. As we headed to the step off area, we were chatting away like old friends. She asked, "Dean, how long have you been doing this?" I glanced at my watch and answered, "About six hours." Her facial expression indicated her disbelief.

I spent the next few minutes convincing her that it was indeed my very first day as Grand Marshal Coordinator. Withrow told me, "A lot of people are intimidated by my position and my title, yet you seem totally at ease. She added, "I predict a long and successful career for you."

Her Grand Marshal duties completed for the day, Ms. Withrow was anxious to watch the parade. We viewed the parade together from the steps of City Hall. Here I observed an Official of the U.S.

Department of the Treasury as she was transformed into a little girl. She enjoyed the parade more than anyone in the park, commenting as Cinderella passed, "Isn't she beautiful!"

Ms. Withrow then offered to autograph a dollar bill for me. She signed her name above her signature. Sound confusing? The Treasurer's signature is on the lower left hand corner of all U.S. currency. I thanked this wonderful lady and assured her that I could not have had a better first Grand Marshal.

I'd like to bring attention to the two individuals that were instrumental in helping me during my early years of Grand Marshaling. The first was Dave Krazit. Dave was my manager at Guest Relations when I came on board in '98. His personal attention and unshakable support provided me with the confidence I needed during this transition. Dave, thank you for believing in me.

Next, the man whose position I moved into, Ray Lait. Ray had been selecting the Marshals for about eight years. My task was to take over for a legend. I once told him that I would have had no larger shoes to fill if I were replacing Walt himself. Everyone loved Ray and Ray loved everyone.

And now here I am 14 years later with people calling *me* a legend and comparing *me* to Walt. Mary Ellen Withrow, I feel your prediction of my "long and successful" career on my first day proved to be very accurate.

Maᴵɴsᴛʀᴇᴇᴛ Mᴇᴍᴏʀy 2

Another Cinderella

"...if you're going to play the role of Cinderella here at Walt Disney World, you'll have to be in our parade today..."

One interesting aspect of my role was that guests would share very personal parts of their lives with me. The following letter from a young lady named PJ is an example:

I'd like to send a special thank you to Dean Gaschler for giving me the opportunity to experience the magic of a lifetime! I recently visited the Magic Kingdom with my boyfriend for the first time this past winter. Upon my arrival, I quickly made my way to Cinderella Castle. All the feelings of youth, freedom, and fairy tales returned followed by tears of happiness in realizing that I was really standing right in front of the castle!

We spotted Dean walking by and asked if he would take our picture in front of the statue of Walt and Mickey. He agreed with a smile and showed us where to pose for a great photo. In our conversation I explained that this was my first vacation here and how excited I was to be in the Magic Kingdom.

As we continued chatting, I explained to Dean that in a lot of ways I'd played the role of Cinderella throughout my childhood. Just like the story, I experienced nonstop abuse and neglect without the fairy tale ending. Throughout my teens, I'd even adopted the nickname 'Cinderella' from my friends due to the poor and harsh treatment I often received. Dean seemed genuinely concerned on what little I'd said about my hard life. Afterward he agreed that, unfortunately, Cinderella and I had a lot in common.

Dean then asked if I planned on watching the parade later that day. I told him I would not miss it for the world. Dean smiled and said, "Well, if you're going to play the role of Cinderella here at Walt Disney World, you'll have to be in our parade today!" He then asked if we would like to be **GRAND MARSHALS** of the parade! I nearly tackled him with a hug and my reply!!

We met Dean at the designated spot later in the day, still giddy and floating in the clouds! He gave me my first set of Mickey Mouse ears, which I will treasure forever, and a certificate for being Grand Marshal. Along the parade route I felt as though I was in a dream. We were being treated as if we were celebrities. Dean was making a total fuss over us. As we rolled down Main Street USA, we felt like a King and Queen.

I cannot even begin to describe the feeling of happiness and exhilaration I experienced. It is a day that I will cherish forever!

I know this is an experience anyone would enjoy, and we feel that Dean made these memories MUCH more special. He spent time chatting with us and even introduced us to many of the parade performers. It seemed he was on a mission to make sure our vacation was the best ever! Well, he succeeded, and I still haven't stopped talking about it to my friends. We cannot describe our parade experience without mentioning Dean's kindness.

Thank you for those kind words, PJ, and thank you for letting me be a part of your special day. I'm so happy to hear that your story had a happy ending.

MAINSTREET MEMORY 3

Video of a Lifetime

Every once in a while a guest would send a thank you note that just said it all. Here's a great example:

Dear Dean, First of all my apologies for this letter taking so long to reach you. I hope you are continuing to make unforgettable memories as you have done for us. It's been over two years since you have selected our family as Grand Marshals. We wanted to let you know all that happened on (and since) that very special day.

When you introduced us to the other family that would be Grand Marshals with us, we noticed the Make-A-Wish buttons they were wearing. Their young son was obviously the "wish" child. As we boarded the fire engine, I was overcome with a tremendous feeling of guilt. I remember praying, "God, why am I here? Today belongs to this young man."

Before we took off, my husband, Rick, asked if he was allowed to use his new video camera. You answered, "Of course, shoot all the video you like." Then off we went. Being in the parade was (and still is) the most amazing thing any of us have ever done.

Our two families became fast friends and we watched the parade with Rick filming the whole thing. We exchanged addresses, phone numbers, etc. On our drive back home to South Florida, Rick said, "I have a great idea, I'll make a copy of the Grand Marshal and parade video and send it to our new friends"...which he did.

Many months later, we received a letter from them. The family wanted to thank us again for sending their son his most prized possession, the video. They said, **"He loved that video and watched it every day-up to and including the day he passed away."**

Dean, I realized then and there exactly why God had us there on that day. We stay in contact with our Grand Marshal friends and exchange cards twice a year: at Christmas and on our "Parade Anniversary" Day. May God Bless You and Your Family. Sincerely, April

Thank You, April...Yes, indeed, your letter says it all.

Mainstreet Memory 4

Great Encouragement

"...my room is covered with Disney Princesses..."

Get ready for a truly amazing story. I met Craig and Jerri Lynn in May of 2007. I'll share a thank you letter I received from them shortly after I selected them as Grand Marshals.

In the 20 years I have known my wife, I have never seen her so filled with joy, cheer and Disney Magic as our experiences on our recent vacation to WDW!! She was captured by the joy of Disney Pin Trading with Cast Members. On our third of five days in the Parks, she had to go back to the Emporium at the Magic Kingdom "for just 30 minutes." She was like one of our grandkids in our matching Disney shirts and her bubbly excitement.

*On Main Street, we met a Cast Member who quite literally changed our lives and we think he deserves some special recognition for the perfect Spirit of Disney he portrays. We are speaking of **"Dean,"** who on May 1st asked my wife if she could wave like a Disney Princess. I realize he does this 365 times a year, but for us it was more than a **Dream Come True!!***

His instructions were clear, yet comical and cheerful. He was prompt in meeting with us later in the day with the first set of Mickey Mouse ears either of us has ever had. Little did Dean know that the very next day was our Anniversary. Dean's Magic is commendable. Sincerely, Craig and Jerri Lynn.

Very kind words, don't you think? Now, here's a follow-up letter I received from Jerri Lynn several months later: (Just a warning...you may want to grab a tissue.)

Dear Dean, I cannot tell you what an honor it was to be chosen Grand Marshal in the May 1st parade. What prompted you to ask two crazy adults, I don't know, and I've been thankful over and over. That unexpected treat has meant more than you can know.

Just after we got home, two of our children announced that they were going to Disney for Christmas and asked us if we would go too. After a short discussion, we decided we would not miss such a wonderful opportunity, even though we had just returned.

Then came our big test! Craig and I were hit by a tractor-trailer and our car was totaled. I have ended up in the hospital for the last two months with a spinal cord injury, making me paralyzed from the waist down. The doctors are doubtful I will walk again. I disagree and believe I will have at least mild movement.

However my room is covered with Disney Princesses and the photos from that Magical Day at Disney. We are still coming back for Christmas! The joy I experienced those five days I spent in the Parks has given me great encouragement. The memories have helped me through countless, difficult, pain-filled days.

So I wanted to thank you for the great gift you gave us. Thank you for our Magical Day and the knowledge that dreams do come true. With special thanks and appreciation, Jerri Lynn.

Since I have no words, I'll share the remarks of our Senior Vice President: "With Disney memories bring an inspiration during tough times, these Guests have high expectations for their next trip. I'm sure we'll be ready to provide them with our legendary service. Thank you, Dean, for leading the way in keeping the Magic alive each and every day!"

MAINSTREET MEMORY 5

Celebrating with Laughter

"...Suppose we had the ability to hit life's rewind button..."

During my career I have worked with many guests that have traveled to Walt Disney World for a family member's final wish. Several years ago I encountered one of the most amazing of these families.

The family consisted of Mom and Dad, an 18 year-old daughter (a college freshman), and her four younger brothers. One of the young men (about age 12) was visiting Disney as part of his wish.

When I met the family for the first time, I noticed an amazing positive attitude complete with lots of smiles and laughter. They were definitely here to celebrate! This continued at the backstage area and all along the parade route. Their enthusiasm was contagious! They were having a blast and so was everyone they came in contact with, myself included.

After the Grand Marshal festivities, I struck up a conversation with the mother. She said, "I hope don't think we're crazy, but we've decided to face my son's illness with laughter instead of tears." She went on to tell me about their "Family Night." (Keep in mind that I've known this family for about an hour or so at this point.)

One evening per month in their home, there is no television and no phone calls. The family gathers to celebrate each other. Part of this special evening is called *Anything Goes,* where there is nothing off limits or out of bounds. Recently during *Anything Goes,* one of the children asked the following: "Suppose we had the ability to hit life's rewind button and could go back to the day before my brother received his diagnosis, and could change it...would we?"

The answer will probably astound you as it did me. Each family member, including the young man stricken with leukemia, voted that they would not change a thing. They were in unanimous agreement that their appreciation of each other and their *"Life Celebration"* could not have come about any other way.

As I said goodbye to this incredible family, I realized what a blessing I'd received by meeting them and what a privilege it was to be part of their Celebration.

MAINSTREET MEMORY 6

A Pulitzer Prize Winner

Mike and Marian Peters attended a charity function and placed a bid at silent auction, then discovered the grand prize was theirs. The couple had won a weekend for four at Walt Disney World. Tracy, their daughter, and her husband, Jude, would be joining them. The package included the Grand Marshals event during their stay. Marian was given my contact information to make arrangements. She and I communicated on several occasions to coordinate their day.

Finally the big day arrived. I met the group and they were excited about the parade. Mike asked if I'd ever seen the cartoon *Mother Goose and Grimm*. I answered that I'd not only seen it, that it was one of my favorites. He said well that's my cartoon and with that, he presented me with a book, a collection of Grimmy cartoons. He had drawn Grimmy on the inside cover and added "Dean is Top Dog," along with his autograph.

The two couples had an absolute blast along the parade route and soaked in every moment of the experience. After the parade there were thank yous and hugs all around. Mike and Marian mentioned that they came to Disney often and would be sure to say hello during their visits. What I did not know is that I'd just met one of the world's biggest kids.

"Mike is the Peter Pan of the cartooning world: he's boyishly charming, good with a rapier, and he doesn't spend a lot of time on the ground. Also, he doesn't seem to want to grow up." —Garry Trudeau, creator of the comic strip *Doonesbury.*

Over the years, I visited with Mike and Marian many times in the Magic Kingdom. I'd learned that *Grimmy* was nationally syndicated and appeared in more than a thousand newspapers nationwide. Mike was a winner of both the Pulitzer Prize and the Reuben Award. Yet, Garry was one hundred percent correct...he was not about to grow up. Mike's energy level makes the Energizer Bunny look like a tired old man.

Practical jokes are also one of Mike's fortes. He's gotten me twice...great jokes, both times. The first time: I'm standing on Main Street and someone pinches my behind! I turn around, and I'm looking at Marian and she's looking at me. Seconds later, Mike pops out of one of the shops, laughing his head off. I turned to Marian and said, "You poor woman, how many times has he done that to you?" She answered, "Thousands."

The second time: Mike had introduced me to Lynn Johnston, his friend and creator of *For Better or for Worse.* We'd had a great time getting acquainted. As we were about to say goodbye, a Disney photographer passed by and Mike wanted a photo of the three of us. The photographer took a quick shot, and Mike asked if he'd take another. Just as the photo was about to be taken, Mike kissed me on the cheek. I have both the "before" and "after" shots.

Peters has a serious side as well. During one of his visits to the Magic Kingdom, I introduced him to a young man who had just returned from his deployment to Iraq. Mike shook his hand and welcomed him home. He then turned to me and asked if I could locate some paper, pen, and a desk. We headed to City Hall and fortunately the VIP room was unoccupied. I located pen and paper and watched as Grimmy appeared on the page thanking the young man for his service. The soldier was so proud of his keepsake!

A former teacher of Mike's offered the following: "You'd better start growing up real soon, because you can't always draw cartoons." Mike, I'll offer a second opinion: "Never grow up, and you can always draw cartoons."

Mᴀɪɴsᴛʀᴇᴇᴛ Mᴇᴍᴏʀʏ 7

Mickey's Top Hat

I met newlyweds Bryan and Adrienne early one morning on Main Street USA. They had not been able to locate the men's "formal" Mickey hat. I escorted them to the Chapeau where we learned that the hats had been discontinued. They were nowhere to be found, including the warehouse. As we stepped outside, Adrienne was nearly in tears.

She went on to explain that the day before, the couple had spent over five hours at the doctor's office and another hour trying to get a prescription for an infection in her eye. They had also cancelled their dinner reservations in Mexico at EPCOT.

I was determined to make the second full day of their marriage better than the first, so I invited them to be Parade Grand Marshals. They agreed and were delighted, yet still concerned that none of their photos would feature Bryan's formal attire. I assured them that I would do all I could to locate a hat for the groom.

Where to start? I asked everyone I could think of about the hat, with no success. I called the Wedding Pavilion, who suggested I try Disney Floral. I contacted Disney Floral and was connected with Jaclyn. After a brief wait, Jaclyn announced, "WE HAVE THE HAT!!" Things were beginning to fall into place.

She then asked if I thought the couple would enjoy an autographed photo of Mickey and Minnie. I answered that I thought they would appreciate anything after what they had endured the previous day. Jaclyn and her team were just getting started. They assembled a gift basket with the autographed photos, champagne, cookies, chocolates, etc. Jaclyn even arranged for the hat and gift basket to be delivered to City Hall.

I felt like Santa as I presented Bryan with his Mickey top hat and the couple with their gift basket. The newlyweds were overwhelmed! We had turned their day completely around. The team at Disney Floral had exceeded any expectation I may have had.

Early the following morning, I left Jaclyn a voicemail thanking her and her team for all they had done. I also shared how appreciative the couple was and all the fun they had along the parade route. Jaclyn relayed to me that she had shared the voicemail with her team.

She said, "It certainly gave us the pixie dust we needed." I'd say that they had provided some much needed pixie dust to this young couple!

MAINSTREET MEMORY 8

One Very Proud American

"Listen With Your Heart"

One morning several years ago, I was approached by a guest named Ed Maloney. He asked me if I knew how the Veteran of the Day for the afternoon Flag Retreat Ceremony was selected. (At that time, this was not one of my responsibilities.) I answered that it was my understanding that the Veteran was selected on a random basis.

Mr. Maloney explained that he had visited the park on numerous occasions and that the Flag Retreat was the highlight of his day. He added that his entire family: wife, children, their spouses, and grandchildren were all in the Magic Kingdom as well.

If that were not enough, he shared the reason for the family reunion. His daughter, April, was fighting the battle of her life and this could well be her final visit to Disney. The entire group had traveled from Pennsylvania to celebrate April and each other.

I asked Ed if he would mind waiting while I checked to see if this could be arranged. I assured him I would do all I could, yet was unable to promise anything. His handshake told me how much he appreciated my efforts.

Backstage, I met with the team responsible for making the selection. After sharing this family's story, I was told to go forward with making the necessary arrangements.

Heading back to Main Street I felt like I was about to give this proud veteran and his family a lifetime memory. I'll let my friend, Ed, tell you in his own words what the ceremony meant to him:

I'd like to tell you about a magical experience I had in The Magic Kingdom at Walt Disney World about seven years ago. I'm a retired Veteran having served 24 years in the Air Force.

Each day in the Magic Kingdom an Honorary Veteran of the Day is selected. At five o'clock in the evening the Flag Retreat ceremony is conducted in Town Square. At this ceremony the flag is lowered, folded, and presented to the Veteran.

I was the Honorary Veteran of the Day December 10, 2005. After the flag was presented to me, an Honor Guardsman announced to the crowd in Town Square in a strong and commanding voice, "Ladies and gentlemen, boys and girls, from Pittsburgh, Pennsylvania, Master Sergeant Ed Maloney, United States Air Force, Retired, Vietnam Era."

The crowd cheered and applauded. I still get chills when I remember this moment. It was a very special moment to me because my wife, children, and grandchildren were all present to witness this. Since then, one of our children has passed.

This experience has strengthened my belief that America is alive and well.

I learned a very valuable lesson from the Maloneys. **Listen** to the Guest...**Listen** with your heart.

Maïnstreet Memory 9

A Kind Heart

"...What Have You Done From The Heart Today?..."

Not all of the amazing people I met during my career were guests. Marvin Smith was my manager at Guest Relations for eight of the fourteen years I selected Grand Marshals. He was extremely supportive of the Grand Marshal program and of me personally. Marvin's motto is *"What Have You Done From The Heart Today?"* Posters asking this were strategically located around the Guest Relations offices.

Marvin always referred to me by one of several nicknames he'd labeled me: "Dirty Dean" or "Deano Cappuccino." I do not remember how all that got started. I felt that if he were pestering me, at least he was leaving someone else alone. Seriously, Marvin has one of the kindest hearts of anyone I know.

Recently Marvin and I were visiting and he reminded me of one of his most memorable Grand Marshal families. I had selected a family that was accompanied by a service dog. I had shared my unusual Grand Marshal selection with fellow cast members, including Marvin and the Guest Relations office staff. This is when I discovered

Marvin's weakness: animals, particularly dogs. He was thrilled about my selection and wanted to know all about the family.

I had learned that the family trained service dogs for future companions. The dog, named Essex, was about to "graduate" and would soon go into full-time service. Giving up this dog was no easy task, as the entire family had become completely attached to this amazing animal. I'd promised a Grand Marshal certificate for Essex and was assured it would become part of his permanent file.

This is when Marvin got involved and I discovered just how kind his heart is. He joined the family and me at parade step off. We were all attentive to the family; yet it was clear to me that Marvin was there to meet Essex. Marvin had brought a "Mickey" food dish, leash, treats, and of course, "doggie" Mouse ears, which Essex proudly wore throughout the entire parade route.

Marvin's career path soon took him to a management position at Disney Resorts. Months later I received a call from the office of Meg Crofton (President, Walt Disney World). The call was from Meg's speechwriter and he had been referred to me. He was looking for a "saying" or a "quote" for an upcoming speech. The quote needed to be meaningful and effective for the cast. I shared Marvin's quote and was told it would be used. Meg's office sent me a framed card with the quote and a personal note from Meg, a gift I will always cherish.

Another gift I will always cherish is Marvin Smith's friendship. He epitomizes the qualities of an effective leader. I was blessed to have his example in front of me for eight years. Thank You,

Marvin...from my heart. And all the best from Dirty Deano Cappuccino.

Personal note from Meg Crofton

Maïnstreet Memory 10

Hugs from the Heart

Early one morning on my way to Adventureland, I met a family that seemed extremely excited to be in the Magic Kingdom. The party included a beautiful young girl traveling in a wheelchair. I greeted them and dropped to one knee to visit with her. I said, "Good morning, and what are we celebrating today?" She answered, ***"MY NEW HEART."***

She went on to explain that this had been a very long awaited trip to Disney World. Her poor health had prevented her from being able to travel from England for several years. Her smile convinced me that it had been worth the wait.

It took about two seconds for the family to accept my invitation to be parade Grand Marshals. After we made the arrangements, I explained to the little girl that this was not free. Her payment, after leading the parade, would be a big hug. She reached down and undid the footrests on her wheelchair. She slowly stood and said, "Dean, I'll just pay you right now"...and gave me a wonderful hug.

That afternoon, the family had a great time on the parade route. I assured them that they had done a great job, yet there was one small problem. They could not imagine that anything had gone wrong. I then explained that the warranty on this morning's hug had expired and I was owed another. My new friend was only too happy to replace her earlier hug.

Much later, I'm guessing two years or longer, I had completed my Grand Marshal duties for the day. Another cast member informed me that I had guests asking for me and pointed to the general area where they were waiting.

As I approached the area, I recognized my "hug" girl. I said, "I cannot remember your name, but I do remember your hugs." As I knelt down beside her wheelchair, we shared another hug and, I must admit, a few tears. I asked her dad how she was doing. He shared that the past several months had been very difficult and the doctors were not very optimistic about the months ahead.

Her father went on to tell me how important it had been for his daughter to see me. This was the last day of their vacation, and the family was certain that this would be her last trip to Disney. They had visited the Magic Kingdom earlier in the week only to discover that it was my day off.

As they entered the park on this day, my "hug" girl turned to her dad and said, "We're leaving for home tomorrow. I have to see Dean today; the trip will not be the same unless I can see Dean."

So many of the benefits I received working with The Walt Disney Company were not found anywhere on a paycheck, yet were priceless. The hugs from this little girl are a perfect example.

Mᴬᴵɴˢᴛʀᴇᴇᴛ Mᴇᴍᴏʀᴩ 11

Kids of All Ages

I love sharing feedback from previous Grand Marshals. I'd like to share two stories from not-so-young Disney guests. First, we'll hear from 100-year-old Foreman's granddaughter, then from 80-year-old Albert.

Hi, Dean! Do you remember Foreman? He celebrated his 100th Birthday as Grand Marshal in October 1998. I'm his granddaughter, and wanted to say hello and tell you Grandpa passed away at the age of 102 years. He was in great health and happiness until the final month of his life.

I want you to know that he watched the tape of the parade frequently and showed it to all his friends. When he moved to a retirement village for the last year of his life, he'd have people in to look at that tape! Once someone even brought their grandchildren to see the 102 year-old man, and they watched his Grand Marshal tape.

He enjoyed his Disney birthday celebration enormously, and I want to say thanks again for making it so special...Barbara

Thank you, Barbara...Wow, 102!! Good for you, Foreman. Next up, Albert, celebrating his 80th in 2000:

After such a memorable birthday over two weeks ago, I have not settled down yet! As a result, I am quite late in sending you and your staff the honors bestowed on me during my 80th birthday.

As I told my daughter, **"My freedom from a POW was the Number One special day in my life, the parade at the Magic Kingdom was next."**

I very much appreciated the courtesy and respect shown to me and my family during this celebration. I would say Disney World is most fortunate to be blessed with your talent and enthusiasm, including the graciousness of your staff... Sincerely, Albert

P.S. Dean, if you ever get tired of that job, you can always head for Hollywood.

Thank you for those kind words, Albert. Hollywood...?? It is fun meeting these "kids" of all ages. Hollywood...???

Maïnstreet Memory 12

I'm Gonna Walk!

In February of 1999 I met a beautiful five year old named Alexandria (Alex) and her mother-to-be Shari. Shari was Alex's foster mom and was in the process of adoption. I had selected the family as Grand Marshals and Alex was so excited for the parade to start. Shari and I helped Alex from her wheelchair into the parade vehicle. Shari asked Alex, "Tell Mr. Dean what you are going to do next Thursday." Alex answered, "I'm gonna have an operation." Shari continued, "Tell Dean what you're going to do after you have your operation." Alex confidently answered, ***"I'm gonna walk!!"***

Shari and I exchanged contact information. After the surgery, Alex told Shari that she was going to go to the Magic Kingdom and was going to show Dean that she could walk. In August I received a card from Shari that the adoption had been finalized in late July. I sent Shari a card of congratulations and sent a Disney storybook to Alex.

Shari shared that the story book had become part of Alex's bedtime ritual. A Disney story, then a quick look at the parade tape with Alex as Grand Marshal. One evening after the story, the parade tape, and goodnight kisses, Alex said, "Wasn't what Dean did outrageous?"

Many months later and just another normal day in the Magic Kingdom...not for long. I entered City Hall and the entire place was buzzing! Where was Dean? When would he be back? I had no idea what the urgency was all about. Finally I connected with Cast at City Hall. It seemed I was the only person in the Magic Kingdom unaware of what was about to happen.

I'd shown up just in time and was instructed to wait, as a guest wanted to meet with me. After just a few moments, the mystery vanished...it was Alex! I went to her wheelchair and gave her a big hug. Shari was in tears, placed me in an exact spot, and then went to Alex's chair. Soon Alex was standing all by herself. Then, slowly, slowly, ever so slowly, a step! Then another! And another! She had done it!! She had walked six or eight steps...all the way to where I was waiting. Waiting with a big hug and tears streaming down my face.

For a few moments everything at City Hall came to a complete stop. Then the celebration began with lots of cheering and applauding. Everyone at City Hall took time to congratulate our Hero. She had done it...and wasn't what Alex did outrageous?

Maïnstreet Memory 13

No Coincidence

You may have heard me say this before: ***"There is no such thing as coincidence, only God remaining anonymous."*** The following series of events will back up that statement.

How I met Barbara: She and her husband were enjoying breakfast outdoors in the Magic Kingdom on a December morning in 2004. I approached them and asked about the chances of leftovers since I was starving. The couple and I struck up a conversation, and before long they were my selection for Grand Marshals.

How I met Sammy: I attended the memorial of my dear friend, Mark, who had passed away after a horrible accident. Sammy was the pastor of the church where this service was held and also a close friend of Mark's. This was August, 2009. I'll now explain the series of events that connected us.

Barbara and her family were "regulars" at WDW, visiting several times per year. Each trip they would locate me just to say hello. We became friends and enjoyed our frequent visits. During a get together in October of 2009, Barbara shared that she would soon begin chemo treatments for cancer. I asked her and her husband to keep me posted on her progress.

To attend Mark's memorial, I'd need someone to "backfill" me. At such a short notice only one person was available, my friend, Fred. I approached Fred asking the favor so I could attend the memorial. Fred said he'd be most happy to fill in for me, but he and his wife were closing on their new home on the same day.

The following day, Fred informed me that his closing had been delayed due to a minor technicality and he'd be able to work for me. Our scheduling manager approved my day off, and I was set. I attended Mark's memorial that Sammy officiated and said so long to my dear friend.

My wife was unable to attend the service. I shared with her how I had felt the genuine outpouring of love for Mark from this congregation. Since we were looking for a church home at that time, we decided to attend a service the following Sunday. We've been attending God's House Orlando ever since.

Sammy and his family surprised me in the Magic Kingdom one day. I asked if they would like to see what I did for Disney. They were most anxious to find out. I then informed the family they were Grand Marshals for this day's parade. At that time, our promotion at WDW was: "What Are You Celebrating?"

Our "normal" celebrations were birthdays, anniversaries, graduations, engagements, etc., etc. Well this day (with Sammy and his family's permission), the Magic Kingdom announced: ***"Barbara's Medical Triumph"*** as its special celebration. Sammy, his family, and I said a prayer for Barbara before parade step off.

I knew precisely the time the parade announcement would happen. I phoned Barbara earlier in the day and told her the exact moment her phone would ring, but not to answer, just let the message go to voice mail. At the designated time, I dialed her number and held my cell phone near a speaker as the parade announcement was broadcast...Barbara still has this message on her phone.

Sammy and his family had a great time during the parade. His daughter, Hannah, even drew a sketch of the Grand Marshal vehicle along with a thank you. I told Barbara and Sammy about each other. On Sundays, Sammy always asked about Barbara and assured me that he was remembering her in prayer. Yet Sammy and Barbara had never met and I wanted that to change.

Barbara and her husband headed to Disney in March of 2010 to officially celebrate her medical triumph. Their stay in Orlando kept them over a Sunday. You guessed it, the four of us headed to God's House together.

The meeting was unbelievable. Sammy and Barbara hugged as if they were old friends reuniting after many years. I guess in a way, that's exactly what they were. Barbara says her memory of meeting Sammy in person and praying with him is a major highlight in her recovery.

So there you have it: A chance meeting on Main Street, a friend's passing, another friend's home closing delayed, Linda and I finding a church home, a family volunteering to honor someone else during a "once in a lifetime" parade announcement, a dedicated church pastor praying relentlessly for someone he's never met, the two having an emotional meeting several years later...a series of coincidences or God remaining anonymous?? You already know what I think....

MAINSTREET MEMORY 14

Honorary Princess

During my years on Main Street, I was involved with many special celebrations. One of the most memorable occurred the month of October, 2005. The celebration was in honor of the first time release of *Cinderella* on DVD. Grand Marshals for this month would be replaced by "Cinderella's Honorary Princess of the Day."

Thirty-one of the luckiest girls on the planet would be selected to travel the parade route in Cinderella's Royal Coach. Riding each day with the girls, ages five to ten, would be their handsome Prince (Dad). Accompanying the coach would be banner carriers, coachmen, and herald trumpeters. An announcement was made along the parade route with the name and hometown of our Honorary Princess.

Each Princess was escorted to the Emporium and was presented with a complete Cinderella costume. In addition, she received a complimentary parade photo, a private meet and greet with Cinderella, and a *Cinderella* movie DVD.

Unfortunately rain prevented one of our Princesses from participating in the parade. Young Chloe had traveled all the way from Hong Kong. Although disappointed that she was unable to ride in Cinderella's Coach, Chloe was extremely excited to receive her gown and accessories.

Princess Brittany created a personal thank you card for me complete with artwork and a beautiful message. Princess Sara sent a drawing and note all the way from Michigan. Many other Princesses sent photos and thank you notes.

Princess Tia from Iowa was featured in three local newspapers complete with photos and her Princess story. Her mother wrote: "I think it is safe to say that just about every little girl in Eastern Iowa is now begging her parents to go to Disney's Magic Kingdom!"

I met Princess Krista on Main Street. Her father, Greg, shared that she had endured over a dozen surgeries due to a brain tumor. Greg and I stepped aside to discuss the possibility of her becoming the Princess of the day. I explained that he would accompany Krista in the coach and her only responsibility would be to smile and wave to the crowd. Her father explained that one of the operations had affected the nerves and muscles that control her facial expression and that unfortunately she was unable to smile.

Greg and I returned to her stroller with a plan. I invited Krista to be the Princess in the parade, but first she had to pass an audition. I explained that I needed to find a little girl that could smile and wave just like Cinderella. First I had Krista wave to me...of course her wave was *perfect!* Next came the Princess smile...again her smile was *perfect!* I'd found my Princess for the parade! A crowd had gathered to observe the audition, and everyone cheered and applauded. Krista was an amazing Princess and the entire Kingdom loved her.

After the parade, Greg said, "Dean, I'll assure you that she will never stop talking about that parade. You cannot see her smile, but I have learned to see the smile in her eyes. She has never stopped smiling today; why would she? This has been the best day of her life!"

MAINSTREET MEMORY 15

Gold Medal Day

Lots of celebrating happens at Walt Disney World for all sorts of reasons. I was a fortunate participant in one of these special celebrations.

I observed a group having a real good time and stopped to find out what was going on. That's when I met Gary and his family and friends. This young man was very excited. He shared that his dad had promised a trip to Disney World if he won a gold medal at the Special Olympics. I asked, "You won a gold medal at the Special Olympics?" Gary answered, "No, I won two gold medals!"

It took me no time to decide that I'd found my Grand Marshals for this day's parade. We met at the designated time and place and Gary was even more excited than before. As we were waiting backstage, Gary asked if he would be allowed to wear his gold medals during the parade, his Mom was carrying them in her purse. I insisted that Gary wear his medals.

Gary proudly wore his medals on the parade route. At the end, he said he didn't know which was more exciting...winning his medals or being Grand Marshal. Gary was also very proud to hear his name and hometown announced over the Magic Kingdom's loudspeakers.

The celebrating continued with Gary and his group when Gary asked me, "Dean, do you like surprises?" I answered, "Sure, who doesn't like surprises?" Gary slowly removed one of his medals and placed it over my head and around my neck.

He had caught me completely off guard. I was totally speechless with a lump in my throat and fighting back tears. It took me several moments to compose myself. I explained to Gary's father what had happened, and that I felt it would not be appropriate for me to keep Gary's cherished medal. Gary's father replied, "My son loves you and that's his way of showing it...keep the medal, Dean, my son knows what he's doing."

So I asked Gary's father (who coaches Special Olympic Athletes), to grab his camera and come with me. I said to Gary, "Let's have your dad take a picture of us together with our gold medals and you can send me a copy."

I've looked at that photo several hundred times over the years...Gary and I proudly displaying **our** gold medals.This young man continues to inspire me to this day. He comes by to say hello when he visits the Magic Kingdom. Gary calls me "his hero." Yet I know *he* is a hero. Read on:

Gary has worked full time at The Christmas Tree Shop in his hometown in Massachusetts for over 10 years. He is a customer greeter because of his cocktail personality.

On a windy winter day in 2009, Gary saved a baby's life in the parking lot. He was gathering carriages in the lot to bring into the store. A carriage was being blown toward the highway by the gusty wind while the mother was busy placing parcels in her car. The baby was in the carriage seat. Gary stopped the carriage from being hit by a truck without worrying about himself.

A policeman witnessed the whole thing and told his supervisor that Gary was a hero. The entire story along with Gary's photo appeared on the front page of the local newspaper. Gary told a reporter that "it was near Christmas and he could not let anything happen to that baby." Our hero was presented a certificate and a medal for his bravery.

Meeting people like Gary and his family during my career has been a true blessing. To be called someone's hero is truly humbling for me. I hope I can continue to earn this title. Gary helps me keep the bar raised high for my own goals...he will always be my Gold Medal Pal.

Gary Bates Jr and Dean proudly display their gold medals

MᴬⁱNSTREET MEMORɣ 16

The Magic Begins With Me

During Disneyland's 50th Celebration in 2005, a "keepsake" entitled, "The Magic Begins With Me" was published. A handful of cast members worldwide were featured. I was very fortunate to be included in this special publication and was able to obtain several additional copies. These were given as gifts to friends and family. One copy was presented to the Seal family from Virginia. You'll be surprised, as I was, how important this book became to this family.

Susan and her parents, Mick and Cindy, were in the Magic Kingdom the summer of 2004, celebrating Susan's 21st birthday and anticipating her admission to dental school. I felt that having them lead the parade as Grand Marshals would highlight the celebration. They could not have agreed more. And, yes, Susan was notified the following day of her acceptance to dental school.

Mick, Susan's father, required open heart surgery in January, 2007. The surgery went well and Mick's recovery in ICU was right on target. A few days later, a device (best described as a temporary pacemaker), needed to be removed from this sensitive area. This is a very delicate procedure and the possibility of a tear in the heart is very real. If this had occurred, Mick's chest would have to be re-opened immediately.

Mick was required to lie perfectly still for at least one hour. His blood pressure would be closely monitored. A drop in blood pressure would indicate a problem. Being calm at a time like this was not easy. Here's where the book became so important.

Susan wrote: "The room was made dark and quiet. We'd brought along a few books and I reached into my bag and pulled out the 'Cast Member' book you'd given us. Mom and I read aloud from that book. Dad listened as we softly reminisced about the many magical memories that the entire Cast at Disney had provided. The hour passed quickly and everything was fine. We wanted to share how, in addition to prayers, you and Disney helped us through a very stressful time."

Over the years I've shared many Magical Moments with the Seal family. Each visit, Susan would locate me to update our annual photo. I was able to surprise Susan with her official "Dr. Seal" Mickey Ears after her graduation. I always look forward to my visits with my friends, Mick, Cindy and this amazing young dentist.

Maᴵnsᴛʀᴇᴇᴛ Mᴇmᴏʀy 17

Christmas Grand Marshals

My friend, Jerred, took over the Grand Marshal duties for me on Christmas Day, 2003. He received a very special gift that day. Let me share Jerred's comments:

Dean, I wanted to pass along this message to you about the Grand Marshals that were selected for Mickey's Very Merry Christmas Parade on Christmas Day.

As I traveled from Main Street to Tomorrowland, I encountered an amazing family. Each person was wearing a Mickey Santa hat and appeared to be the very definition of the perfect Disney Family. I approached them and began to inquire about their day. During this conversation they were smiling, laughing, kidding with each other, etc. I knew I had my family so I asked if they would be staying for the parade. When I asked if they would be interested in being in the parade as our Special Grand Marshals, the kids literally erupted. I began taking down the family's information and setting a meeting time and place. I noticed Mom beginning to tear up; she put her sunglasses on when she noticed her young son watching her. I thought nothing of this since tears of joy are a fairly common occurrence after being asked to join the parade as Grand Marshal.

After I had taken the information I had only traveled a short distance when the father of the family stopped me and asked if any part of the show would be strenuous. I answered that there were only a few steps up a short stairs to the parade float. Their main responsibility would be smiling and waving, something they had already proven quite capable of doing! He smiled and replied that he just wanted to be sure because the two youngest children were **both** terminally ill and this could potentially be their last Christmas. The kids had wanted to meet Mickey for Christmas and Mom and Dad had made that happen. I assured him that there was nothing strenuous involved with the experience, yet if he felt the children would not be up for it, that I would understand. He said there was no way they would miss this once in a lifetime event!

Later that day I met the family at step off. By this time one of the younger children had started getting tired and was now riding in a wheelchair. I presented the family with their Mickey hats and certificate. Mom began reading the certificate to the children but had to stop when she started to choke up. Dad took the certificate and completed the reading. The float arrived and the family climbed aboard and away they went. All along the route, the family was greeted by other Guests waving and shouting Merry Christmas. At step down I assisted with unloading the family from the float and showing them to their reserved parade viewing area. I shook hands with each of them, thanked them for their participation, and wished them Happy Holidays. Mom told me that I had "made this the most special

Christmas ever" and that she could not thank me enough.

Dean, I am sure you have hundreds of stories just like this one. I hope you understand why I feel that stories like these deserve to be passed along. I've always felt like we are all the masters of our own fate, but I can't help thinking that something else had a hand in selecting this family on this day. I will never forget Christmas Day 2003 and the experience that the Grand Marshal provided for this very deserving family. I feel certain that they won't soon forget it either because for that brief moment no one was ill and happily ever after was their reality.

Sincerely yours, Jerred

As I said earlier...I believe Jerred was the one on the receiving end of that special Christmas gift.

Mainstreet Memory 18

Back to School Fun

Disney Magic is everywhere. Debra from Massachusetts shared how her and her family's special Grand Marshal day wound up in a college classroom. Debra wrote:

Last summer as I attended a graduate course at my local college, I shared a very special time with my classmates.

The first class we were asked to share a special event unique to each of us. I knew my event was the best! As my turn approached, I listened to many interesting stories from my classmates including the birth of a child, skydiving, travel to exotic places, etc...etc...

When it was my turn to share I confidently said, I was a Grand Marshal at a Disney Magical Moments Parade. Furthermore, my family and I traveled in a fire engine and waved to thousands of people as they lined the sidewalks of Main Street USA.

To my satisfaction, I heard a classmate say, "You got me beat...how did you manage that?" My response was, "I guess we were at the right place at the right time." Also, my husband was wearing a Donald Duck shirt...who can resist that?

Thanks for the Disney Memories and we hope to return soon.

Thank you, Debra. So great to hear how special your Grand Marshal day was and thanks for sharing with your class. Although I can't speak for your professor, I give you an A+.

MAINSTREET MEMORY 19

A September 11th Hero

There are hundreds of heroes from 9-11 whose efforts and bravery have touched us all. John DePalma is one of these heroes. John is a County Officer in New Jersey who responded to the attack on the Twin Towers on September 11, 2001.

John arrived at Ground Zero via police boat and stayed for four days and nights as part of the search and rescue mission. Unfortunately, his efforts were to no avail, as he was not successful in finding any survivors. Then, on September 14, DePalma was injured and was hospitalized. For the next six months, John required physical therapy to rehab a tear in his knee. He also spoke with crisis counselors, trying to cope with all the death and destruction he had witnessed.

DePalma felt a trip to Disney World might offer a positive distraction and headed to Florida in the spring of 2002, all the while wondering: "What if I still don't feel any better? Suppose the nightmares and flashbacks continue?"

When I met John in the Magic Kingdom, I had no idea what he'd been through. I saw his NYPD ball cap and t-shirt and his knee brace. I asked and he responded that he had been part of the rescue efforts. I remember telling him that it wasn't every day that I got to shake the hand of a real hero! John and his friend, Joe, were thrilled when I invited them to lead our parade as Grand Marshals. I spread the word throughout the cast that a hero would be leading today's parade. Many cast members responded with handshakes, hugs, and thank yous after being introduced to DePalma.

As the pre-parade festivities began, I walked the parade route in front of the Grand Marshal coach. I was firing up the crowd, telling them that a hero was on the way. Along the route, a lady with a small boy told me, "This child's father is stationed in Afghanistan." I remember her shouting "thank you" to John, and him shouting "thank you" back to her.

After the parade, DePalma told me that he would be back later in the week to share photos and more stories. We met several more times during that week and decided that it would be a good idea to continue communicating. A few weeks later, I received a letter from John telling me that for the first time since the tragedy he felt that he was making real progress. He'd been in a much better frame of mind and felt that his trip to Disney had been his best possible therapy.

Fast forward to June 14, 2012: John surprised me on my last day working at Disney. He was seated in the vehicle when I headed backstage for my turn to be Grand Marshal. My friend had flown in to surprise me and had caught me totally off guard. He, then fired up the crowd for me as I rode along the parade route...sound familiar? He also did an amazing job as DJ at my retirement party the following evening, yet another fabulous surprise!

To this day, John DePalma and I have remained good friends. He is still a Deputy Sheriff in New Jersey, a talented DJ, and a part-time Disney Cast Member. I hold this young man in high regard and truly admire his energy and enthusiasm. As I said earlier, it is not every day that I got the chance to shake the hand of a real hero, and I'm very honored I had the chance to shake this hero's hand.

Mainstreet Memory 20

Small World in Church

"...this shows the depth of emotion..."

Today, I want to introduce you to James, a courageous and energetic 11 year old. I met James in 2005 during his visit to Walt Disney World to fulfill his "wish." He had been battling childhood cancer for some time before I met him. James and his family were very active in their church and James sang in the junior choir.

I'd like to share parts of a letter I received shortly after their visit:

Thank you so very much for giving our family the special honor and thrill of being Grand Marshals of the parade. It was an exciting experience, one we certainly never expected. It was the highlight of our trip which we will remember and treasure forever.

James has endured 60 weeks of chemo for his brain tumor that has slowly robbed him of some of his sight. His twin sister, Emily, is perfectly healthy and I think would gladly shoulder some of the burdens her brother must carry. When we were informed that James' situation met all the requirements of Make-A-Wish, we shared the news with the entire congregation. **We were going to DISNEY WORLD!!**

On the Sunday before our trip, the junior choir sang "Jesus Turned My Life Around" and "It's A Small World." The whole congregation joined in on the chorus to send us off. In a solemn, old-style Presbyterian Church...well, this shows you the depth of emotion!

We feel that God puts certain people in your path at different times in your life for various reasons, that hopefully will become apparent later. We were blessed to meet you and appreciate your good nature and sensitivity. You spoke so lovingly of your Make-A-Wish friends and acquaintances. The work that both Make-A-Wish and Disney does is so much more than just a holiday. It's hope and joy and the knowledge that people you've never met can care and share so much.

Maïnstreet Memory 21

A Military Salute

Each day prior to the Share a Dream Come True Parade, certain Magic Kingdom guests are selected to serve as Grand Marshals. They are made to feel like celebrities when their names are announced over the public announcement system as they ride along the parade route. Their "job" is to smile and wave to the crowd.

As Grand Marshal Coordinator, I selected the majority of these participants. During the 2005 holiday season, I participated in one of the most incredible events of my entire career at Disney.

It was the idea of Walt Disney Company CEO Bob Iger to select military families to serve as Grand Marshals from Thanksgiving until New Year's Eve. Instead of selecting the Grand Marshals in the Magic Kingdom, I traveled to Shades of Green Resort each day during this program.

Meeting these military families was just amazing for me. I discovered that they are very humble with a very strong family bond. Additionally, I noticed a very strong faith. Most days, the parting words from these families were, "God bless you."

As a result of my interaction with these Guests, I received the following letters:

I wanted to thank you again for making our Christmas even more special than it already was. I never dreamed that being Grand Marshal would be such an emotional experience. To see the appreciation and gratitude of the Cast Members and the people along the parade route brought me to tears. (U. S. Army Specialist)

Never in our wildest dreams would we have thought of such an honor. Words cannot explain the feeling that we experienced as we rode along the parade route. We received applause, waves, thumbs-up, salutes, thanks for serving...what a thrill! For Disney to honor the military is fantastic. (U. S. Air Force Airman-Retired)

Bryan, a Magic Kingdom Parade and Fireworks Entertainment Manager, added the following:

When Major Huffman was told that he and his family would serve as Grand Marshals, he turned to his wife and said, "All the bombing and shelling I went through was worth it for this."

Each day Dean brings these special people to us and each family allows us to become part of their lives, if only for a moment. That moment is why we are all here.

Allow me to share the most perfect salute of all. An especially moving moment for me personally was witnessing an elderly veteran along the parade route. As our military Grand Marshal family approached the area where he was seated in his wheelchair and the announcement was made, he slowly stood and saluted.

It was obvious that it was extremely difficult for this elderly gentleman to rise from a seated position. It reinforced in me the common bond the active and inactive military men and women share.

Boxing Legend George Foreman with Dean at the Harmony
Barber Shop

Maĩnstreeţ Memơrỵ 22

Princess Haley

"We were uplifted to a place that is hard to describe." Ken, Haley's Grandad

I met Haley and her family on Main Street USA. They were very easy to spot, as the entire party of ten were wearing matching bright red "Haley's Pals" sweatshirts. It was evident that this group was here to celebrate! The family consisted of Haley, her mom, dad and brother, uncle and aunt, two cousins, and Mimi and Pap (grandparents).

Haley's mom, Jill, and I struck up a conversation and she shared the following: When Haley was 5, a golf ball-sized brain tumor was discovered pressing against her spinal cord, obstructing the flow of her spinal fluid. Three days later, a team of neurosurgeons saved Haley's life. Now, two years later, Haley and her Pals were in the Magic Kingdom celebrating her recovery from a second surgery to remove a recurring tumor. In 2011 alone, Haley had 89 doctor appointments!

Jill gathered the gang after I told her that I had a surprise I wanted to share with everyone. They all nearly jumped out of their skins when I invited them to be our Grand Marshals for the day. I had also learned that Haley's granddad, Ken, was a Vietnam Veteran. Ken was asked to honor us as our Veteran of the Day at the Flag Retreat Ceremony, and tearfully accepted.

Later, at parade step off, Haley and her Pals were treated to a Royal Meet and Greet by many of the parade characters and performers. (My thanks to the amazing Magic Kingdom Entertainment Cast.)

Haley and her family lit up the parade route throughout the Magic Kingdom Park. *"This is the BEST day of my life!"* exclaimed Princess Haley.

"The feeling we experienced being in the Parade is indescribable. We were overtaken by emotion and reached a feeling of extreme bliss." Jill-Haley's Mom

Later that day, Ken proudly participated in the Flag Retreat Ceremony in Town Square. Haley and the rest of the gang observed from a special viewing area near the flagpole. I joined the group to view the ceremony and celebrate with this proud United States Army Sergeant.

Several weeks passed and I received a letter from Ken. In his letter he said, "The pictures taken at the Flag Ceremony will be a permanent part of my service collection. I was honored to be Disney's Veteran of the Day." He further shared that the honor bestowed upon him at the Magic Kingdom that day was one of the biggest highlights of his life. And he added that it was the first time he'd been "recognized" since returning home as a Vietnam Veteran!

A big day for Haley, her Grandad, and their pals, wouldn't you agree? It has been nearly a year since this magical day in the Magic Kingdom. Since then, I've remained in contact with this special family. Haley has recovered from a successful third, yes, **THIRD** brain surgery. This beautiful eight-year-old

Princess continues to amaze with her enthusiasm. She loves to play soccer and her last report card was straight A's. Haley and her pals have uplifted **me** to a place that is hard to describe.

Mainstreet Memory 23

Her Name Is K-e-i-r-a

A guest once asked what a normal day was like for me at Disney. I answered that I really didn't remember having too many "normal" days. I'll share an example. How many days have you gone to work and become directly involved in naming a baby?

I met Corey, Elizabeth, and their son, Jared, along with Elizabeth's mother on Main Street and enjoyed visiting with this family. I remember Elizabeth proudly mentioning that Corey was a firefighter. It was difficult not to notice that a new member of the family would be arriving soon. I invited the family to be Grand Marshals for this day's parade and they immediately accepted my invitation.

Each day after my selection, I would collect information from my Marshals...family names and hometowns for parade announcement and first names to personalize their Mouse ear hats. Having all the necessary info from this family I mentioned, "I see we have another passenger traveling with us today. If we have a name for him or her, I'll have that name sewn onto an infant-sized hat."

Now I know what you are thinking: "Good move, Dean"... "attaboy, you Magic Maker"... "that's how you Disney Cast do things." Not so fast. Corey looked at Elizabeth and Elizabeth looked back at Corey.

Apparently this discussion had taken place before without an agreement on a name for their daughter. I was feeling just a tad uncomfortable. So what to do now?

I offered the following, "This is not the child's birth certificate; it is just a set of Mickey Mouse ears. I'll get the ears for the child and you can have the name sewn on at a later date." This is when Corey announced, "Her name is Keira, spelled K-E-I-R-A." And that was it...the baby was named! My guess is this was Elizabeth's choice for the child's name and spelling. She immediately went into tears and hugged her husband. Additionally, I'm proud to announce that I have been designated "Honorary Grandad" for Keira.

So there you have it, just another "normal" day for me at Disney.

Maïnstreet Memory 24

Princess Kenzi

Hundreds upon hundreds of requests to participate as Grand Marshals crossed my desk during my career, none as touching as the one I'll share now. This request was forwarded from the Grand Floridian Resort. Tissue alert!!

The Grand Floridian and Walt Disney World have literally been a "life-saver" to our family. Our daughter, Kenzi, was diagnosed at birth with a rare kidney disease. She received her first transplant at fifteen months and managed to grow into a happy child in spite of feeding tubes, medications, blood draws, physical and speech therapies, and multiple surgeries.

On our first visit to the Grand Floridian, Kenzi was in good health and had a most memorable visit. During this trip, we met Larry and he took us for a ride in his old fashioned car. To Kenzi, this was more exciting than anything else in the world. From that moment on, Larry was her hero! After we returned home, she spent hours and hours watching our family video of Disney World and her special friend, Larry.

A few months later Kenzi became critically ill, lost her transplant and went back on dialysis. Fighting for her life, we promised she would return to Disney as soon as she was able. In May 2002, we returned to the Grand Floridian for nine days; toting our dialysis machine, boxes and boxes of medical supplies, medications and a stable (but ill) daughter. Larry was at the door when we arrived and made us all feel very special! He arranged for balloons and a personal note and photo from Mary Poppins (Kenzi's absolute favorite character) to be delivered to our room. Additionally, Mary Poppins magically appeared at Alice's Tea Party and Cinderella's Royal Breakfast during Kenzi's visit. It was a truly fabulous experience!

Little did we know what an important role our trip to the Grand Floridian would play in keeping Kenzi alive. She was scheduled for her second transplant on October 30, 2002. Knowing that Walt Disney World is the best medicine for Kenzi, I wrote Larry and asked him to send her a note. Not only did Larry send a beautiful letter...during our three month stay in Minnesota (1,000 miles from our home in Texas) Larry arranged for photos and notes to be sent from all the characters. We were overwhelmed at the generosity and support! Kenzi pointed them out to every doctor, nurse, housekeeper, or passer-by. She felt like a Disney Princess!

The transplant went well and we expected to return home by Thanksgiving. Unfortunately, Kenzi contracted an infection that left her life in the balance. For 37 days she laid critically ill in a hospital bed, watching Thanksgiving, Christmas, and New Years pass her by. Often she would ask, "Mommy, when I get well, can we go back to Disney?" She was always told "Yes" and she would smile and keep fighting.

We arrived home in January and immediately booked the Grand Floridian for early April. Once again the infection reared its ugly head and we were rushed back to Minnesota. We rescheduled our Disney trip for late April, but were forced to cancel. Kenzi became so ill, the medical team thought we had lost her. She underwent six more surgeries, removal of her abdominal wall, complete paralysis for six days, two weeks in I.C.U., breathing machines, countless drugs with horrible side effects and spending Easter, Mother's Day, and Memorial Day gravely ill and away from home.

When Kenzi rallied (to the surprise of all), she wanted to know when we were going to the Grand Floridian to see Larry and "Can I be at the front of the parade?" (i.e. Grand Marshal). The doctors concur that it was her dream of returning to Disney World that gave her the strength to survive!

Our family has been home for two months. Kenzi started school last week and becomes healthier every day. We are moving full speed ahead to arrive at the Grand Floridian for the Thanksgiving holiday. We are confident that we will make this trip as "three is a charm" and we have so much to be thankful for!

As our family knows, the Grand Floridian cast members truly perform miracles! As parents, it is very difficult to watch our daughter struggle to sustain her life. We would move mountains to indulge her dreams. Knowing of no other way to fulfill our daughter's fantasy of being "at the front of the parade," I am turning to our miracle workers for help. If there is any way to arrange for Kenzi to participate in a parade, my husband and I would *be eternally grateful. We truly appreciate all that the Grand Floridian has done for us in the past and can hardly wait to arrive for Thanksgiving. Thank you for sharing the Magic!*

On November 29, 2003, Kenzi realized her dream to be in the car in front of the parade, as she and her family served as Grand Marshals. Kenzi's mom sent me a thank you and added: ***"You're an angel!"***

Maïnstreet Memory 25

A Special Walk Down Main Street USA

Several chapters in this book make reference to the Cast Member publication produced in 2005 entitled: "The Magic begins with Me." The following is the story that featured Dan Hodess and me.

On Saturday, September 9, 2000, I selected Dan Hodess, his family and friends to be the Grand Marshals of the Magical Moments Parade. Dan is a Deputy Sheriff of Broward County, Florida. About two years ago, while assisting a motorist, Dan was struck by a car and lost both of his legs. Through numerous surgeries and countless hours of therapy, Dan had a goal of walking the Disney Theme parks and playing golf on a Disney course. He was here celebrating his miraculous achievement.

Dear Dean Gaschler, On behalf of the happiest Grand Marshals you'll ever encounter, I wish to thank you for taking such good care of our gang!

During our first conversation, you told me that you would do your best to make my dear friend, Deputy Daniel Hodess' time in the park unforgettable! Your commitment to doing just that was quite evident! He had an incredible time, as did the rest of us. I believe we all sprained our faces from smiling so much!

Like so many other people, I am a huge Disney lover. I have been going to Disney World since the day it opened. BUT, nothing will equal the enormous feeling of pride I had on September 9, 2000, when I saw Danny's smiling face while waving to the layers of people standing along the parade route.

Nothing will match the look of surprise when he heard his name booming over the loud speakers as we turned down Main Street. And nothing will ever compare to the joy on his face when we reached the end of the line and were greeted by the beautiful harmony of the Dapper Dans and the clever wit of Miss Tabby. Those shared memories will stay with me forever.

Dean, I understand that both the Dapper Dans and Miss Tabby really went out of their way to visit our party. I would greatly appreciate it if you would pass along a sincere thank you to all. They are all to be commended for making Danny's day special!

Last, but certainly not least...Dean, you are an absolute gem! It was definitely my pleasure meeting you. You are a gracious gentleman and in my humble opinion, you are the 'perfect man' for the job. That smile never left your face...I think you enjoyed the experience almost as much as we did. I hope our paths will cross again someday. Either way, you will always hold a special place in my heart for what you did for all of us, but most importantly, Danny.

Warmest Regards, Mary Del Borrello

(The following is from Dan Hodess):
I would like to take this opportunity to thank you for what you did for my wife, my friends and myself. As you were made aware of some of the incidents that occurred to me, you made my hard

work worthwhile. It took a lot of little steps to make the trip possible for me. Part of my goal was to show my wife that we could still do things that are enjoyable and that we can still have fun.

I wish to commend you and the staff that took the time to share that moment of our honorary positions with us. You made it a very special occasion...one that we will cherish for a long time. Thanks again to you and all the staff involved.

Grand Marshal Roy Disney, Jr. with Mayor Christopher George Weaver

Mainstreet Memory 26

A Grateful Nebraska Family

Hello Dean! As I am sure that you meet so many grateful families, I will try to describe our encounter so that you may remember meeting us!

Our Family (Jorge, Leah, Abbey and Lindsey) met you on Main Street just outside of one of the art shops in early December, 2009. We were in search of prop phones that guests can pick up and listen to fun conversations. After chatting with you for a few minutes, you saw my husband's Nebraska Medical shirt and we discovered our "mid-west" connection. Then you gave us the surprise of, well, a lifetime and asked us to be the Grand Marshals for the Parade. We were even able to add my folks, making this a true family event.

Needless to say, being Grand Marshals was simply; magical. But what you don't know and what is so funny to our family is the story behind our trip. If you have a few minutes I will regale you!

Two and one half years ago I was diagnosed with breast cancer and had to go through the whole shebang...surgeries, chemo, radiation, yadda yadda. As you can imagine, as a family, we were pretty shaken...especially the girls. So, before my treatment Jorge and I surprised them with a trip to Walt Disney World. It was so great, they thought we were going to a KU football game, it was the best surprise and they never saw it coming.

We laughed, over-ate and closed the parks each night. We celebrated being a family and knew that together we could overcome any obstacle. It was pure family time and I was so grateful for that diversion. When we got home, I got back to the cancer business and am now cancer free. God is good. And the best part is that when I think about that particular time in our lives I can't help but think about that surprise trip to Disney and riding Expedition Everest four times in a row, getting stuck on the Pirates of the Caribbean ride and hearing "dead men tell no tales" for fifteen minutes straight, and watching my beautiful daughter's faces as they had no worries. It was magic for us.

So there we were in December 2009 and are headed back to celebrate NOTHING. No first year cancer free celebration, no nothing! It was wonderful. But, we did like the idea of surprise, so each family member planned something in secret. However, the girls needed my help with their surprises (sleigh ride at Wilderness, balloon ride at Downtown Disney) and Jorge giggles too much so I had him fess up to me. The result was that I knew everybody's surprise. But then we met you and did you get us all! It was the perfect SURPRISE!

You and the staff at WDW may see Disney as a place of employment, a job...but for us and so many people like us, WDW is magic. A trip to Walt Disney World is having your kids all to yourself for a week, it is having your husband hug Winnie the Pooh, it is really believing in fairies. And we have you and your staff to thank for that. Keeping magic alive can't be easy, but trust me when I say it is so much appreciated.

I will let you go now...I hope that 2010 is wonderful for you and all that you care for. We may be back in October. We will stop by to say hi. Enjoy the Huskers t-shirt, not sure if you can wear it being a "Kansas Guy" but it comes with much love.

Take care and have fun spreading the magic!

Leah

Leah's mother, Jean, added the following:

I wanted to personally send a quick note to let you know that Fred and I were thrilled to be Grand Marshals in early December. Every time we look at our video, we relive the whole event. Leah and I keep talking about the chances it all happened. It will be a lasting memory and we owe it all to you. Your genuine love of people just radiated from you and is quite catching.

As a Mother and Father we witnessed firsthand the great impact breast cancer has on a family...not just the person, but the spouse, children and parents. We could only hope that after going through that process our daughter would find wonderful things happening to her.

Leah and her family battled cancer head on and now we move forward...enjoying each day and learning how to appreciate someone such as yourself. We hope to see you again soon. Thank you so much.

With the greatest appreciation, Jean and Fred

Maïnstreet Memory 27

Princess Waverly

I met Waverly and her family on Main Street USA the morning of April 29, 2011. Waverly is almost five years old and has been through more than almost anyone I know. She was born at twenty-seven weeks and barely weighed two pounds. She has had three brain surgeries (the latest in January 2011), and surgery on her spine, heart, and stomach. She is unable to walk and can barely speak.

Yet, there she was lighting up Main Street with her beautiful smile! As I was visiting with the family, Waverly became distracted by the trolley show. Waverly's father lifted her from her wheelchair and handed her to me! The music, the dancers and their colorful costumes had totally mesmerized this little girl. As I held her, this precious child literally fell in love with the dancers.

I motioned to one of the performers to meet us at the Car Barn after the show. We all met for lots of photos and hugs. Waverly was having so much fun and the dancers were making her feel so special! Someone asked Waverly's father how they knew me...he answered, "The Good Lord sent Dean to meet Waverly."

One of the trolley operators asked if our new friend would like to meet Charlie, a beautiful

Percheron. I asked the family if Waverly would be frightened by this huge animal. Quite the contrary, she loves horses and riding is part of her therapy. So I got to witness another magical moment as Waverly and Charlie became friends.

During this time, I made arrangements with the family to join me for their Grand Marshal experience. That afternoon as I escorted them backstage in preparation for the parade, many of the cast approached the Grand Marshal vehicle to say hello to Waverly. She hugged them all...some more than once.

The parade stepped off, and Waverly was the star of the show! I joined the family to watch the parade pass the Grand Marshals at step down. Again, the whole gang waved and blew kisses to Waverly from the parade route. The Entertainment Cast in the Magic Kingdom gave Waverly and her family a once in a lifetime memory.

I'm sure Waverly will always remember this day, I know I will. In closing, I want to tell this family...*I think the Good Lord sent Waverly to me.*

Mainstreet Memory 28

Eric and Lisa Massey

United States Army Major Eric Massey shared his greatest achievement in his 22-year military career:

"I was in charge of deploying 176 troops for duty in Iraq...and I brought all 176 of them home!"

An accomplishment indeed! First of all, may God bless each and every one of our military men and women stationed anywhere in the world. Next, thank you, Major Massey, for bringing all of your troops home. We all salute you. Their job was to provide security for the voting locations for the first elections in Iraq's history. Can you imagine?

Eric and his wife, Lisa, were in the Orlando area in February of 2012 visiting their friends, Rick and Cheryl. Rick was battling cancer and his prognosis was not good. Their son, Ross, served under Major Massey in Iraq. I knew when they would be visiting the Magic Kingdom, and invited Eric to serve as Honorary Veteran of the Day at the Flag Retreat Ceremony. He immediately accepted.

Linda and I were invited to join Rick and Cheryl and the Masseys for dinner that evening. This is when I got to visit with Eric and Lisa and learn about their life-changing event. Lisa is this super-charged ball of energy and her perpetual smile is contagious. She's just fun to be around. Eric has a great sense of humor, is very outgoing and does not know a stranger. Together they are an amazing couple.

About thirteen years into their marriage, the couple was attempting to adopt. Their dream was to adopt one or two children of toddler age. After miles of red tape, it appeared that two boys, ages four and seven, would be available. Hold everything...yet another sibling, a nine year-old sister, surfaced. The children had been "paired off" with two of them living together at different times and different locations. The three had NEVER lived together!

Eric and Lisa went forward with the adoption. Lisa shared, "A brown van stopped in front of our house, our three children (each with just a duffle bag) got out of the van, and that was it." Many adjustments needed to be made...the Massey's had gone from zero children to three in just a matter of minutes, and the kids were finally all together under the same roof...for good.

About six months after that brown van drove away, it was time for the Masseys' first family vacation...you guessed it, the gang headed for Walt Disney World!

Mainstreet Memory 29

The Stamp Family

Ashley Stamp was a gifted downhill skier. There was even conversation that she had a good shot at making the U.S. Olympic Ski Team. This rising star had been on skis since she was two years old. She and her family lived in Steamboat Springs, Colorado, the perfect location for her passion. Then, while warming up for a race in Vail, Ashley was involved in an awful accident and lost her life at the age of thirteen.

Aaron and Kelly, Ashley's parents, and younger sister Samantha were devastated by their loss. Months later, Samantha was nearing her tenth birthday and the family was undecided on how to celebrate. After weeks of struggling, it was decided that the Stamps were heading to Ashley's favorite place on earth, Walt Disney World.

Ashley visited WDW for the first time when she was just twenty-two months old. On that visit, she met the "love of her life"...Mickey Mouse. Many Disney vacations to California and Florida followed, creating many cherished memories for the Stamp family. In August of 2005, Aaron, Kelly, and Samantha were headed to Orlando for the first time as a family of three...what was Disney going to be like without Ashley?

The family arrived early in the evening and checked into their room at Port Orleans Riverside. An energetic Samantha learned that the Magic Kingdom would be open until midnight and wanted to go. Aaron and Kelly knew it would be difficult, and decided to go sooner rather than later. They went to tackle the unknown head on.

Upon their arrival, the Stamps discovered very short lines at many of the Magic Kingdom's attractions. Samantha headed straight to Big Thunder Mountain. Now I need to explain that when Ashley rode any sort of roller coaster, she insisted on riding in the very front, no matter how long the wait. A cast member asked the Stamps the size of their group. For the first time that answer was "party of three." The cast member led them to the front row. Since there was still time before using their Fastpass for Splash Mountain, they decided to ride Big Thunder again. Our friends were directed to the opposite loading area. Again, the ride attendant directed them to the very front row!

So the trio headed to Splash Mountain. As they approached the loading area, an attendant asked, "How many?" Once again the answer was "three" and once again they were escorted to the front row! Kelly was convinced that Ashley was with them on their trip and was helping them get to the front row, minus the long wait. As they cruised along, a large wave came over the side of the boat and the group got soaked. Kelly immediately yelled, "Thanks, Ash" and they all laughed hysterically!

Kelly wrote, *We walked around the Magic Kingdom for a while longer then decided to head back to the Resort. As we rode the bus back to Port*

Orleans I smiled to myself and thanked Ashley for easing us into this trip and letting us know she was with us. It truly was a "magical experience" beyond my dreams! We walked to our room hand in hand and I realized that we had made the right choice in coming to Disney World and that Ashley was right here with us.

I met the Stamps the following morning in front of Cinderella's Castle. When I asked if it was just the three of them, I really struck a nerve. Kelly and Samantha began to weep and walked away in opposite directions. Aaron stood there tearing up. I'd never had a family respond in this manner. I apologized to Aaron, yet had no idea what I had said to offend them. Aaron explained some of the details regarding Ashley and understood that I had no way of knowing.

Kelly and Samantha joined Aaron and me and I apologized to the ladies. I then explained that my intent was to invite them to participate as parade Grand Marshals. Determining the party's size was part of the information I needed.

Ashley was given credit for directing me to meet her family, and they agreed to be the Grand Marshals. As we became acquainted, I realized what a special family I had just met. Kelly gave me a photo of Ashley and her website address.

During the parade, Ashley was up to her old tricks as we all got rained on. We all connected and I knew I would be seeing the Stamp family again. Over the years, we have become very good friends. Several years after we met, Samantha became a big sister as Ashlyn and Ashton joined the Stamp family.

I posted the following on Ashley's website:

Hello Ashley, I'm writing from your very favorite place...Walt Disney World. I work in the Magic Kingdom. I had the pleasure of meeting your beautiful sister and your wonderful parents. During our visit, they shared some of your amazing stories...we also shared some laughs, some tears, and some very special hugs. I have a photo of you that your family gave me here on my desk.

I plan to keep it there so you can continue to be a source of inspiration to me. I have lots of family and friends in Colorado. Who knows, maybe one day I'll make it up to Steamboat to visit your family. Your Friend, Dean

P.S. Say "hello" to Walt for me.

Dean and his wife, Linda. Dean's retirement party

Maïnstreet Memory 30

A Poetic Tribute

Have you ever had anyone create a poem in your honor? Neither had I...and a safe bet was that this would never happen. Yet, at my retirement party I was surprised with a beautifully crafted gift!

Some background: My daily routine allowed me to interact with much of the talent and entertainers in the Magic Kingdom. I became friends with singers, dancers, musicians, and stage and parade performers. One very talented group was the "Citizens of Main Street USA." These "themed" characters would stroll along the street in their gorgeous costumes initiating guest contact. It was always a pleasure to greet or be greeted by these gifted individuals.

My friend, Holland Hayes, is a member of "Citizens." I've known this versatile gem of a performer for many years. He has shared his amazing talent on Main Street for over 15 years and has a huge guest following. What prompted him to write a poem about me, I'll never know. Allow me to share what I consider a masterpiece:

Walt Disney lived on Main Street
At Disneyland he dwelled
In a lamp above the Firehouse there
They say his spirit's held

He walked along our Main Street here
Before the streets were laid
With Guests he never strolled here
Never sang or laughed or played

We walk in Disney's footsteps tho'
We know it cause we've seen
We walk WITH Walt whenever
We walk down Main Street with Dean

Walt Disney lives in Disneyland
His spirit still aglow
In the window, in that lamp
He's still part of The Show

At Disney World now
Walt won't be as near as often seen
At Disney World Walt Disney
Lived on Main Street inside Dean

As you leave your own Legacy
And take your final bow
Remember Walt now lives in us
Dean Gaschler showed us how

When I read this, I find it hard to believe that he managed to connect me with Walt Disney... *"A Humbling Tribute,"* indeed! The fact that this creative artist took the time to recognize me makes this gift even more special. A close friend of mine shared that he feels so touched by this poem that he reads it daily.

Then, to top it all, the presentation! During the entertainment portion of my retirement party, Holland takes the stage and reads the poem to everyone in attendance. You literally could have heard a pin drop. The perfect gift in the perfect wrapper.

How do I go about thanking someone for such a gift? What I've written is an effort to do just that, yet I feel it falls short. So, Mr. Holland Hayes, I'm positive that when Walt looks down on Main Street USA and sees you at play, he is very pleased...we both thank you.

Mainstreet Memory 31

Warming the Hearts

"There is no such thing as coincidence, only God remaining anonymous!"

The definition of "exuberance" is joyful enthusiasm. This word also describes Ashley Imbrogno, from Mentor, Ohio. Ashley and her mother, Karen, joined together to form *"Warming The Hearts."* This non-profit organization is responsible for making and distributing thousands of blankets to Cleveland area nursing homes, hospice centers, senior centers, and Ronald McDonald Houses, to name a few. Today, at age 15, Ashley has earned a resume that would make anyone proud.

When Ashley was 5 years old, she was hospitalized for a reaction to a childhood immunization. During her stay, Ashley was given a teddy bear by another patient. She named her bear "Hope." Her idea began while working with her grandmother on a fleece blanket, a Christmas present for her father. "Warming The Hearts" was born in 2006. To date, Ashley's organization has raised over *$50,000 and has distributed over 6,000 blankets!*

I met Ashley in 2010 during Disney's "Give-A-Day, Get-A-Day" Celebration. Ashley's organization was recognized by Disney during this "Volunteer" Program. As fate would have it, the Magic Kingdom was also honoring these volunteers as our Grand Marshals. Ashley, her parents, and her grandparents were a perfect fit.

While visiting with the family after the parade, Ashley asked if I knew anyone who would like one of her blankets. (Does she EVER stop working?) I replied that my mother suffered from arthritis and was always cold. So she asked, "What sort of blanket do you think your Mom would like?" I explained that Mom was immobile and confined to her home. Most of her day was spent praying her Rosary and watching Mass on TV. Ashley suggested a "Mother of Guadalupe" blanket and I agreed. My Mother cherished Ashley's thoughtful gift, and now so does Mom's friend, Andrea, the "keeper" of the blanket since Mom's passing. You can learn more about Ashley and her organization at: www.warmingthehearts.org

The company that Karen works with partnered with Disney on this Volunteer Promotion. While at a conference, Karen spoke with a Disney representative. She shared that during the 'Give-A-Day' project, Warming The Hearts had received over 1,600 blankets, many with personalized notes. What an amazing connection!

So, Miss Ashley Imbrogno, I tip my hat to you. Keep going...you are something VERY special. I'm thankful that our paths have crossed. I've heard that there is no such thing as coincidence, only God remaining anonymous! You gave my Mother a gift that she cherished, yet the two of you never met. Your small gift was huge! So was "Hope." Thanks for sharing your exuberance. I love your joyful enthusiasm.

Recognition for 15 years of service

Mainstreet Memory 32

Kids of All Ages

"...When Dean invited them to lead the parade, Betty started to sink to her knees..."

I'd like to share my meeting with Betty and Chuck in 2008. Jeffrey, then a Merchandise Manager at the Emporium, introduced us. The following is his description of their day shared in an email to Jeffrey's entire team:

Today Holly and I had the opportunity to engage ourselves with a wonderful couple from Venice, Florida. Betty and Chuck were visiting us to celebrate Betty's 86th birthday. The couple was also celebrating their 39th wedding anniversary. As we were talking with them, we asked Chuck about his colorful shirt. Chuck likes to draw Disney characters, so he draws them on his shirts and then Betty embroiders them so they stand out. Chuck's shirt had several different characters and he even had characters drawn on his shoes.

Chuck and Betty have been visiting our parks yearly since 1999. Chuck said one of the many reasons they come to Disney is that he feels that the world has become a very cold place, so he and Betty come here to escape the reality of it and immerse themselves in our Magic. WOW!! During our conversation about making people feel good, Betty shared with us that she bakes about 2000 cookies every Christmas and gives them to homeless shelters and other agencies in need, and still doing it at age 86!

I excused myself for a moment during the conversation so I could get one of our "happy birthday" ears embroidered for Betty. I ran to the Chapeau and they quickly stitched her name in hot pink to match the hat.

On my way back, I saw Dean from Guest Relations and asked him to come and meet our new friends. Dean introduced himself and started making small talk; he immediately knew he had his Grand Marshals! He was just as impressed with this colorful couple as we were. It was impossible not to fall in love with these folks.

When Dean invited them to lead the parade, Betty started to sink to her knees-we thought maybe she was going to pass out, but quickly recovered. Both Chuck and Betty were excited beyond words. Dean also mentioned that they would be riding in Mickey's limo...you would have thought they had just won the lottery. Dean gave them the instructions where and when to meet and explained what would happen.

As the pre-parade motorcade came down Main Street, we had seven of our Cast Members out waving and cheering for Betty and Chuck. When they saw us, they started waving and pointing at us...the Chuck and Betty Fan Club! We followed them to the Firehouse and had a quick meet and greet with them. As we were about to part, Betty shared with us that she is a certified clown with the stage name of Tootles. What a way to end our magical day! A very special thanks to Dean who made all of this happen.

Jeffrey, thank you for those kind words. And I believe the Cast at the Chapeau and the Emporium, along with the "Fan Club," and Holly and yourself made lots of Magic happen for this special couple. Let's call it a team effort.

Dean near his "office" at City Hall in Town Square

Maïnstreet Memory 33

Ground Zero

We all remember where we were and what we were doing the morning of September 11, 2001. Nicole was at Ground Zero when this horrific event took place. Just a few weeks later, I had a chance to meet her and her boyfriend, Anthony, in the Magic Kingdom. Here's their story.

Anthony and Nicole had been planning their vacation for several months. After Sept. 11, they struggled long and hard with their decision to continue with their plans. They agreed that the trip was much needed and somehow Nicole was able to get over her new found fear of flying.

Upon their arrival in Orlando, the couple observed guests and cast members wearing "American Flag Mickey" pins. They searched high and low for at least one of these special pins. They were not to be found...anywhere. We were selling out of these pins the moment they hit the shelves. Anthony was not about to give up on his quest to find this special pin for Nicole; he knew it would mean the world to her.

Anthony noticed the pin I was wearing and asked if I knew where he could find one. I need to mention now that the pin I was wearing was given to me by a New York Firefighter. A prized possession indeed. Anthony mentioned the importance of the pin, since Nicole had been at Ground Zero. We became friends immediately and I was just happy to be talking to her, thankful that she had survived.

Anthony and Nicole instantly accepted my Grand Marshal invitation. After making the necessary preparations for parade, I was off to find a pin for Nicole. I asked every cast member about a pin...no luck. Then it hit me: Merchandise!! And here's where my luck changed. One of our merchandise managers had an extra pin she was saving. After sharing Nicole's story, the pin was mine.

Nicole's hug was more than enough thanks as I presented her the pin. I introduced the couple to everyone I could and all were genuinely happy to meet them. Both loved the parade and at the end there were thank yous and photos. Then it happened: I looked off to my right and there stood the firefighter that had given me my cherished Mickey pin. I motioned him to join us and introduced him to Nicole. They hugged and there was not a dry eye in the group...a truly amazing moment.

As we parted, I heard my friend tell Nicole, ***"God Bless You and God Bless America..."***

Mainstreet Memory 34

A Magical 21st Birthday

Guests often inquired about writing to share their Grand Marshal experience. When they did, I'd ask them to try to explain what it **felt** like to lead the parade. The young lady that wrote the following letter did just that.

My first trip to Walt Disney World was in 1988. I was four years old. Like most four year olds, my memory of the vacation was very limited; just a few fleeting glimpses of smiling faces. One unusually vivid recollection, however, was the Main Street Parade. I had fallen asleep and was awakened by lively music, brightly colored floats, and an array of Disney characters prancing down the street. My parents recall my eyes being as large as saucers. Never before had I seen anything like it. Even behind the rope, I still felt like I was part of the show. Mickey waved from atop the float, and I swore that he was waving just to me. From that moment on, I was hooked. Every following vacation had to be to Disney.

I had the privilege of being raised by Disney fanatics. My bedroom was filled with Disney stuffed animals and Minnie Mouse graced my comforter and curtains. As a family we went to see every Disney movie on the day of its release. We purchased videos (and later, DVDs) the same day they were made

*available to the public and, of course, watched them
that very night after dinner.*

*My trips to Walt Disney World as a child were all
about seeing my idols...Minnie Mouse, Robin Hood
and Alice. Even though I outgrew my fascination
with characters, we continued to make yearly
pilgrimages to Orlando. I started to appreciate other
aspects of Disney World. I saw the amazing talent
in the stage shows, the detailing in the buildings,
the optimism of the Cast Members, and, of course,
there was the food. I noticed things beyond the
typical hype, the small nuts and bolts that made the
whole system work. I was experiencing not just what
Disney World was, but what it was meant to be. The
emotions, the smiles, the anticipation, the family
having fun despite being in 90 degree heat...this
was what Walt Disney World was intended for. This
was what Walt Disney imagined and brought to the
world. I realized that I had gone from a girl awed
by Minnie Mouse to a woman awed by Walt Disney.
The feeling was phenomenal. Going to Disney World
was, now, not so much about having fun myself,
but watching other people have fun. This was a
place where kids could let loose, parents could relive
their childhood, and everyone could bask in the
sweet rays of magic. How did Walt Disney ever find
a way to bring these feelings to life?*

*He used approaches like parades, and a parade
would, unknowingly, be the thing that changed my
21st birthday from average hoopla into an
unforgettable adventure. I had wanted to turn 21 at
Walt Disney World, so on my birthday, we entered
the Magic Kingdom expecting to have a day filled
with multiple trips to Pirates of the Caribbean,*

pictures, and too many Dole Whips. We headed up Main Street and, while I was interacting with characters, my Dad started talking with a very official-looking Cast Member named Dean. Dean explained that his job was to find the happiest people in the park each day. Well, we must have looked pretty happy, because Dean announced that we'd be leading the Share a Dream Come True Parade as Grand Marshals.

*Us? Grand Marshals? It seemed too good to be true, and it still had not sunken in as we waited for the parade to begin. Dean met us at the parade gate and introduced us to our parade car...one from Walt's own collection, a car Walt had actually driven and ridden in. As I sat in the front seat by the driver, emotions came over me. Walt Disney sat here, right where **I** was sitting. I was in awe. We were each given mouse ears with our name embroidered on the back and the parade began. The gates opened and we began riding along the parade route, smiling and waving to all the people in the crowd. Everything was so dream-like. There we were, seeing everything from Walt's viewpoint. I saw children eagerly anticipating the parade, and adults suddenly perk up, smile and wave as we passed by. The music was playing, people were smiling, and I realized that, at that moment, I was part of the magic.*

That day, The Magic Kingdom was full of magic...not the magic conjured up by stage shows and fireworks, but real, honest magic. I was given the opportunity to have an experience that I will always treasure and certainly never take for granted. My 21st birthday unfolded into an event that only Disney could have created. Years from now, I can tell the story of how I rode in Walt Disney's car and led the Share A Dream Come True Parade down Main Street USA. My friends will probably assume that I made a deal with some Cast Member. I'll always know that it took a little pixie dust and good, old fashioned Disney Magic to make my dreams come true.

Thank you, Dean, and all the Cast Members at the Magic Kingdom for creating such a wonderful program. You truly touched my heart and made my birthday extra special. Bless you all! Sincerely, Susan

Did I have the best job or what! Thank You, Susan, for sharing your Magical experience and how it felt to lead the parade that day. Quite a 21st birthday...

Maïnstreet Memory 35

Dominick's Christmas

Several years ago, on a mid-November morning, a fellow cast member from Fantasyland approached me on Main Street. She asked if I had made my Grand Marshal selection for the day. I told her I had not. She said, "I know we don't do things this way, BUT...I've befriended a family who has a wish and a prayer. All they want is to have another Christmas with their son, Dominick."

I answered, "You're right, we normally don't do things this way; where are they?" She led me to one of her attractions where we met Dominick (age 5), his sister, and their parents. They were overwhelmed when I invited them to be Grand Marshals. Dominick's condition was not mentioned during this meeting.

That afternoon as we were waiting at a backstage area the entire family was anxious and excited. The kids were having a ball showing me how they were going to smile and wave along the parade route. As I was chatting with the parents, I felt a tug on my slacks. I looked down and there was Dominick looking back at me with his big, beautiful, brown eyes.

Dominick then spoke the words that I will never forget...*"Mr. Dean, did you know that pretty soon I'm going to be an Angel?"* How I kept from "losing it" then and there, I'll never know. As I watched the family along the parade route, I thought to myself...what a wonderful way for these parents to handle this, what courage they must have!

After the Grand Marshal event, Dominick was getting pretty tired. I asked the family to wait and I'd be right back with a stroller for the kids. Dominick's dad insisted on accompanying me. Along the way, he told me something he wanted to share with every cast member at Walt Disney World.

He said, "One of the things I love most about my wife is her smile. Ten months ago, when we were given Dominick's diagnosis, my wife stopped smiling. Since we've been here, my wife has been smiling again... you folks that work here are miracle workers."

After Christmas and New Year's I saw my friend from Fantasyland and asked about Dominick. She shared that she had recently heard that Dominick was still with us. It warmed my heart to know that Dominick's family had gotten their Christmas wish.

Mainstreet Memory 36

The Fortner Family

While strolling down Main Street USA on the morning of August 21, 2003, I had no idea I was about to meet a family that would become very close friends. Our meeting was not "love at first sight." In fact, our first meeting was a bit rocky. Cheryl Fortner and her son, Kiel, were enjoying (or trying to enjoy) breakfast at the Main Street Bakery. They were seated outdoors, and the guests at the adjoining table had three young boys that were totally out of control. The parents were paying no attention to the kids. One of the boys was chewing up his muffin then spitting it out on the sidewalk where the birds were enjoying a feast.

Cheryl was livid! How could these kids be acting like this in **her** park? And why in the heck wasn't I (the official-looking Disney guy) **doing** something? I said hello and walked toward the Castle. As I headed back down Main Street, I noticed Cheryl and Kiel. I began the conversation with, "I feel exactly as you do about those guests, yet the children were not physically harming themselves or another guest." That had calmed her a bit, but she was still pretty upset.

I told the pair that maybe I could help improve their day. The look on Cheryl's face said, "Just how are you going to do that?" When I mentioned Parade

Grand Marshals, I suddenly had her attention. Cheryl and Kiel were most anxious to hear what I had to say. They agreed that this would indeed improve their day and had a great time on the parade route.

The following day my new friends came back to the Magic Kingdom for photos and a quick hello. Cheryl said she could not wait to introduce me to her husband, Rick, and Kiel's brother, Ross. A few months later she got to do exactly that. Kiel was a college student in Daytona and Ross was in the Army.

The family purchased a condo near Disney property. Since Rick's work required lots of travel, Cheryl spent more and more time in Florida. That meant more time at Disney, and she always came by to say hello. By this time, the Fortners had met Linda and we were all becoming friends. One evening while we were visiting with Cheryl, she mentioned she had always wanted to see the Magic Kingdom "after hours" when the park was empty.

I spoke with some Main Street personnel to get clearance, then contacted Cheryl. I asked if she'd be interested in seeing the park "before hours." She was ecstatic! We met early one morning for a quick visit before park opening. During the tour, she handed me her video camera and her flip-flops. I had no idea what was about to happen. My only clue was Cheryl said she was about to do something she'd wanted to do since she was a little girl. With the camera rolling she did not one, but several cartwheels on Main Street. Her lifetime dream had come true. Kiel was in the park one day and informed me, "Dean, you've got to stop spoiling my mother." I replied, "Never."

Ross was deployed to Iraq and Rick, Cheryl, and Kiel visited Disney during the Christmas holidays and vowed they'd spend next Christmas at Disney with Ross. In December of 2005, the Fortner family was honored as the "Military Family of the Day" in the Magic Kingdom to celebrate Ross's return from Iraq.

Not all I've shared with the Fortners over the years has been cartwheels and laughter. When my father passed away in July of 2010, I immediately flew to my hometown in Kansas. My daughter (also named Cheryl) and her family were driving to Kansas from Colorado. I grabbed my cell phone to check their progress and pushed a "Cheryl" button. I'd pushed the wrong button and phoned Cheryl Fortner. Although she was busy, Cheryl took time to find out "how I was doing." Her words were so soothing and comforting. Just what I needed at that time...I had not dialed the wrong number after all.

Later in 2010, Linda and I were strolling on Daytona Beach. My cell phone rang and it was Cheryl...I could tell she was upset. She opened with, "Dean, 2010 has struck again." Then she shared the news that took me to tears. Rick had been diagnosed with cancer in many of his major organs. Nothing that the doctors had to say was encouraging.

Rick fought with everything he had and Cheryl was beside him every moment. The boys rallied around their father. The entire family was the model of strength. In March of 2012, Rick lost his battle and I lost a friend I loved. Cheryl asked me one day, "Do you know where I was that day I called you to let you know about Rick?" I said, "No, I have no idea." She said, "I was sitting in my car...in your driveway."

So here we are nearly ten years later. Kiel has a great job and is doing well. Ross and his wife, Kelly, were married on August 21, 2010, on the day I met Cheryl and Kiel seven years earlier. In May, 2013, Cheryl will become a grandmother for the first time.

The Fortner Family has become part of our family and vice-versa. We have celebrated many major holidays together. Recently, we were at Cheryl's home and someone proposed a toast. I tapped my glass with Cheryl's and said, "Here's to unruly kids!"

Maïnstreet Memory 37

The Amazing Claire

During my twenty-one years with Disney I met literally thousands and thousands of guests. Very few have left such a memorable and positive impression as a young lady named Claire from Liverpool, England.

I was introduced to Claire in 2002, via a letter that her parents, Gary and Karen, had written to Disney sharing the family's upcoming visit. The letter somehow ended up on my desk. Gary asked if something special could be arranged for Claire. After learning what Claire had gone through, I was most anxious to meet her and try to make some magic for this family.

When Claire was twelve years old, her parents noticed that she seemed to be walking with a sort of "tilt." When she was examined, Claire was diagnosed with a condition called scoliosis. They'd never heard of the term, and were about to learn far more about it than anyone would want to. Briefly, the symptoms of scoliosis include a curvature and/or a rotation of the spine. According to her physician, Claire could very likely have to face a worst case scenario. Titanium rods needed to be inserted, one on either side of her spine.

Claire's first surgery took place in February of 2000. The rods ran the entire length of her back and her spine was drawn as close to them as possible. The procedure lasted eleven hours and Claire was immediately placed in I.C.U. Many months of pain and anguish followed during her recovery. Claire endured and insisted on taking her school exams, passing them all.

In late 2001, Claire suffered a setback and it was decided that another procedure was necessary. This would involve the removal of seven ribs from her back. Claire was scheduled to undergo this surgery in December of 2002. Gary and Karen knew that a trip to Walt Disney World would work wonders for Claire and the family headed for Orlando in July of 2002.

Gary shared their arrival date and a Florida phone number to contact him. I phoned the first day of their stay to make arrangements to meet in the Magic Kingdom. Claire, now sixteen, was unaware that any of this was happening. The following day, Gary and I met...it was like saying hello to an old friend. Karen and Claire soon joined us. I introduced myself to Karen then turned to Claire and said, "You must be Claire; I've heard so much about you."

The previous day's parade had been cancelled due to rain. The family I had selected was able to return on this day. I'd asked if they would mind if Claire accompanied them. They cheerfully agreed. Claire's face was a picture when I asked her if she'd like to ride in the parade. There was not enough space in the vehicle for Gary and Karen to accompany Claire; yet I think they were more excited than anyone in the Magic Kingdom!

Claire thoroughly enjoyed being in the parade, and I was also able to introduce her to my friends, the Dapper Dans, our Main Street barbershop quartet. My wife and I joined Claire and her parents for dinner and enjoyed a very special evening. Linda and I now have dear friends in Liverpool. Gary shared that the trip had gone a long way in taking Claire's mind off what she was about to go through in December. She was telling everyone about her experiences at WDW.

It so happened that the Dapper Dans were headlining a barbershop show in Sheffield, England in September. Gary and I were able to coordinate a huge surprise for Claire. The quartet drove to Liverpool and spent the evening visiting with the family. The family attended the performance in Sheffield and shared that the evening was fantastic and that the Dans stole the show.

Claire was admitted two weeks before Christmas and had seven ribs removed. The aftermath and her recovery lasted much longer than expected. During this time, Claire was preparing to sit for her A Level exams for college. The college arranged a special chair and room, and she passed all ten of her A Levels! We asked Gary and Karen if Claire could come to Florida for a visit. Our thinking was that a little sun time, pool time, and Mickey time may help with her recovery. Unfortunately, her surgeon felt it unwise for her to travel.

In 2004, my friends returned for another Disney vacation. We were able to spend lots of time together, including going out to dinner two evenings. During this visit, Gary declared, "Dean is Claire's silver lining."

Claire graduated from college, studying Human Resource Management. She served an internship in New York City in 2008. While in the States, Claire flew to Orlando for a long weekend and stayed with us. We had a celebration for her at our home. The quartet that surprised her in England was in attendance. It was a very special evening for all.

It hurts me that our dear Claire is awaiting a date for yet another major surgery. There are issues with some of her metalwork and a spinal fusion. Gary shared that she is handling this news with courage and integrity. In fact, Claire is thankful that something can be done. Her major fear during the exams and MRI was the doctors informing her that they'd be unable to do anything.

I wish the best of everything for you, Miss Claire...you deserve the brightest silver lining ever!

Maínstreet Memory 38

Face to Face with Mickey

This is as close as I feel comfortable going "behind the scenes" at Disney. You'll understand what I'm saying shortly. Later, we are literally going to get inside Mickey's head.

First, I want to introduce you to Diana. I met her just a few months ago through a mutual friend. She is a former cast member. Diana and I never met while we worked for Disney. We may have passed each other while at work without knowing...one of Diana's work locations was the Magic Kingdom.

Diana is a talented performer and singer. We try to catch her when she performs in our area. During her career at Disney, one of her roles was in Entertainment. She became very close to Mickey. In fact, sometimes they were inseparable... (wink, wink).

Recently, Diana and I were reminiscing about our "Disney Days" and sharing stories. She shared one of the most touching Cast experiences I'd ever heard. OK, so here's the part where we are going to get into Mickey's head. Here's Diana's (and Mickey's) story:

*Mickey was scheduled for a VIP meet and greet for a very special Guest (yes, **ALL** the Guests are special).*

He had been informed that the three-year-old girl that he was about to meet had been born without sight. The little girl also wanted Mickey to talk to her, and we all know that Mickey is unable to speak during these meetings.

*So Mickey got down on one knee and let the little girl come up to him. She approached Mickey so soft with her arms out in front of her. When she got close enough to touch Mickey, the little girl began to shake and started to cry...she was **SO** excited!! These were not tears of fear; she was not afraid of Mickey, these were tears of joy and excitement.*

All she could say was, "Mommy, Mommy, I'm touching his ears...Mommy, this is Mickey's nose...Mommy, Mommy, I can't believe I'm touching Mickey!" And Mickey held her tight and let her take as long as she wanted. No one was going to rush her. Mickey was hers for as long as she needed.

All Mickey could hear was, "Mommy, Mommy, I can't believe I'm touching Mickey's face." She touched every part of Mickey's head and face, crying tears of joy the entire time.

Thank you, Diana and Mickey, for sharing this amazing story. I cannot help but think that those minutes spent with Mickey changed her life forever.

I shared with Diana the day I met a father and son in Town Square. Dad was holding his son (I'm guessing the boy was seven or eight years old) and letting him "feel" Roy Disney's face on the Roy and Minnie statue. This boy was also sightless.

After a nod of approval from the father, I introduced myself to the young man. I asked if he knew whose statue this was. The youngster wasn't sure, but guessed it was Walt Disney. I told the young man that he was very close, and that it was Walt's brother, Roy.

Was I in for a surprise! This young man was an encyclopedia on Disney. He began to share facts about Walt and Roy and Disneyland and Walt Disney World, many that were new to me. I could have visited with this guest for hours. The rest of the family soon appeared and were anxious to head toward the attractions. Mom shared that her son loved anything and everything relating to Disney and thanked me for sharing with him.

So thanks again, everyone...you've opened my eyes!

Ross at Ft. Bening after returning from tour in Iraq with his scarf.

Mainstreet Memory 39

A Scarf for Ross

During my twenty-one years at Disney, I received many unusual requests. I'd like to share the following example:

Dean, I have a huge favor to ask of you. Our son, Ross, is with the 82nd Airborne Division in Iraq. This is the first Christmas he will not be with us. He loves the red and white scarves that the Cast Members wear during the Holidays. I would love to get one to send to him in Baghdad. The scarf will help him feel connected to us...and to the Magic Kingdom. I'd appreciate any help you could offer.

I remember thinking after I read this request, How in the world am I going to locate one of those scarves? It just so happened that a good friend of mine, Chris, had recently transferred from Merchandise to Costuming. I shared the guest's story about their son and the scarf. Chris assured me that he would look into the matter.

Several weeks passed and, to be honest, I had pretty much forgotten about the scarf. Then, one morning, Chris appeared on Main Street and asked me to step backstage with him. He displayed a scarf that was no longer "good show quality," yet the perfect scarf for Ross! Chris said, "Dean, take the scarf and send it to that young man in Iraq!" I thanked him profusely for what he had done for

Ross. The following day the scarf was headed to Ross's parents, then on to Baghdad. A few weeks later I received the following thank you from Ross's parents:

Dean, I wanted to thank you for getting the scarf for me to send to Ross. When we learned that Ross was leaving for Iraq right after Thanksgiving, I lost my Christmas spirit.

I could not stop thinking about him. My baby was halfway around the world doing a dangerous job.

Disney World is our favorite family vacation place. So I thought, what better way to help Ross feel that connection than sending him something special from Disney. You and your friends helped us achieve that goal, and I cannot express how much it meant to us.

Disney means so much to us. It's more than just a place we visit. It's the people we meet, the laughter we share, and the memories that will last through the generations of our family.

Ross cannot wait to come to Disney to meet you and thank you in person. Cast Members like you have become friends that we look forward to visiting whenever we are there. Your generosity and compassion in helping our family is something that we will treasure forever.

Many months later, I was honored to meet this young man. Ross and his family were visiting the Magic Kingdom...welcoming their hero home. He was part of the U.S. deployment responsible for securing the voting locations allowing the first elections in Iraq's history.

So what began as a very unusual request from friends I'd met in the Magic Kingdom turned out to be an opportunity for me to meet a hero. Did I mention that the young man to whom I'd sent a red and white scarf also came home with two Purple Hearts?

MAÎNSTREET MEMORY 40

A Determined Ballerina

"One day I'm going to dance in this parade!"

Some of the most inspirational stories I've heard are cast members making such an impression on someone that the person becomes a cast member as a result. I had worked at Disney for over 15 years and wondered if this were ever going to happen to me. When it finally did, I think you will agree that it was well worth the wait. Here's Kaylee's story:

When Kaylee was three years old, her parents took her to see a ballet. She stood on her chair with her eyes fixed on the performers. That was it. Kaylee was going to dance ballet! By the time she was a senior in high school, Kaylee was sure what she'd be doing with her life, and it all revolved around dance.

Then it happened, Kaylee suffered an ankle injury that jeopardized her entire career. Our lovely ballerina had no Plan B, no safety net. She was a recent high school graduate and had not turned in a single college application. What's next? Of course, there was only one answer...*"I'm going to Disney World!"*

I met Kaylee and her Mother on Main Street in 2006. She asked if I would mind taking their photo and I agreed. The girls shared that they were celebrating Kaylee's senior trip. They were ecstatic when I invited them to be Grand Marshals!

After the parade, Kaylee and her Mom assured me that they'd had an amazing time. They said that they felt as popular as Mickey and Cinderella along the parade route. We shared a picture, a hug, and a goodbye. Story over, right? Not quite. Kaylee and I were destined to meet again. I had no idea I'd impacted this young lady enough for her to pursue a career at Walt Disney World.

Fast forward two years: I'm on my lunch break in the cast break room, having a sandwich, glancing at a magazine. A pretty young lady with long red hair stops at my table and says, "Hi, Dean. My name is Kaylee; do you have a minute?" I answered, "Sure, it's nice to meet you, Kaylee. What can I do for you?" Kaylee continued, "We've met before, but it was over two years ago so you probably don't remember, but you're the reason I'm here."

For the next few minutes Kaylee poured her heart out to me. During our first meeting several years prior, I'd had no way of knowing about her shattered dream. She shared that the ride she took along the parade route had changed her life. As the car passed the castle and headed up Main Street, she told her Mother: "One day, I'm going to dance in this parade!" By this time, we were both in tears. We exchanged phone numbers, a hug, and agreed to keep in touch.

Kaylee works on Main Street very near the spot where I first met her and took the photo of her and her mother. She says that while the rest of the cast has their "Uncle Walt," she has her "Uncle Dean."

This young lady continues to be an outstanding cast member with many goals and aspirations.

Several months ago Kaylee was involved in an auto accident and re-injured her ankle. Even with another setback, Kaylee has never taken her eye off of the prize. She is strengthening her ankle post-injury and is determined to audition for a dance position in the very near future. My bet is that one day she will dance in a Disney Parade.

Kaylee shared one of her favorite quotes. It's from a man that I know is as proud as I am to be Kaylee's uncle:

All the adversity I've had in my life, all my troubles and obstacles, have strengthened me...You may not realize it when it happens, but a kick in the teeth may be the best thing in the world for you—Walt Disney

Linda and Dean celebrate the Holidays at Magic Kingdom
Guest Relations Christmas Party

Mainstreet Memory 41

"Happy Like This"

Princess Alex (age 8) and Princess Emma (age 6) visited the Magic Kingdom in June of 2011. They were accompanied by King Drew and Queen Mandy and were visiting from the far-away land known as Arkansas. After years of symptoms, in 2009, both girls were diagnosed with a rare genetic disorder, Pantothenate Kinase-Associated Neurodegeneration (PKAN). Their condition is terminal.

The girls have both experienced significant declines in their health. Through it all, they smile and are so very happy. If Alex felt that someone was having a down day, she would smile and say, ***"Be happy like this!"***

A friend, Nancy, gave me the heads up that the family was on the way to Disney. It was determined that because of the girls' frail condition and the intense Florida sun, they would not be suitable candidates for Grand Marshals. We needed another plan so I started asking for help. I partnered with Emily, Buck, Pablo, and James and along with an amazing act of kindness from Jodi, we soon had the situation under control.

Here is how the visit to the Magic Kingdom unfolded for the two Princesses. I'll start with Pablo:

Emily, Dean, and I met the family in City Hall. Emily presented them with Princess Ears and autograph books. Both Princesses were wheelchair bound, so to them, these were their chariots. The excitement on Alex and Emma's faces was priceless! In spite of their situation, their happiness is very inspiring. Drew and Mandy were so very appreciative and asked us to pose with the girls for a photo. Drew gave us a warm handshake and Mandy gave us a heartfelt hug.

James had arranged for the family to tour Cinderella's Castle Suite at 3:00 PM. Cinderella was busy at that time with her parade duties and unable to meet her special guests. Emily and Pablo delivered gifts from Cinderella for our young friends. Buck was the party's tour guide and wrote the following.

Emma and Alex were so sweet and it was a pleasure to show them the Suite. They did not know where we were going until we got to the doorway. I could see in their faces how excited they were and how special this was for them. They were unable to vocalize their thoughts, yet I could see from their smiles and expressions that they knew exactly where they were.

With Emily, Pablo, and Dean's help, we had arranged for signed photos of Mickey and Cinderella to be placed on the nightstands for the girls, along with plushes of their favorite characters, a signed Disney book, and lots and lots of Pixie Dust.

Thank You to anyone who helped Alex and Emma's dreams come true. I just opened the door to the Suite...I just opened the door...

My teammates were not done yet. Jodi, an Operations Manager with Magic Kingdom Entertainment, had planned a "super meet and greet" with the girls' favorite characters for the following day. I had worked many events with Jodi and had a saying, "Whenever I work with Jodi, something good happens." You'll understand after you read the following:

I was anxious to meet Princess Emma and Princess Alex. Prior to their arrival, we found out that Alex's favorite character is Cinderella and that Mickey is Emma's favorite. Both girls were bursting at the seams when I came to see them and had no idea what to expect!

I explained that I had some very special friends who had heard that the Princesses were in the park today. I asked if they would like to meet my friends who had been waiting...and waiting...and waiting for them to arrive. They were so excited! Although the girls could not verbally communicate, the sparkle in their eyes and the smiles on their faces said enough. They were beaming with anticipation of what was to come.

I had invited Cinderella, Prince Charming, Fairy Godmother, Mickey and Minnie to come to meet the girls. I had provided them with information about the girls, their family and their vacation up to that point so they could incorporate it into their interaction. Cinderella knew that Emma and Alex had visited the Castle Suite and had received gifts "from her" upon arrival. She seamlessly asked how they liked visiting her castle and if they enjoyed the beautiful gifts she had left for them. Prince Charming could not have been more poised, standing slightly back from Cinderella yet making sure to kneel by the girls and call each of them "Princess." Fairy Godmother presented the girls with Princess gift bags containing little goodies including small Princess purses filled with Fairy Dust. She tied all the stories together perfectly, referencing their "carriages" (wheelchairs), asking if they had seen the stepsisters (Emma thought they were "mean") and even going as far as to wipe Alex's little mouth when she became too excited.

Although Mickey was Emma's favorite character, Minnie quickly became the favorite since she was wearing one thing that no little girl can resist...a pink dress! Emma grabbed on to Minnie's hand immediately and wouldn't let go. The girls were thrilled with the characters and couldn't get enough. There were plenty of smiles, a few tears from Mom and Dad, and they continuously reached out for the characters to get hugs, hold hands, or just a moment of their time. I escorted the family to their VIP parade viewing area. The characters went out of their way to blow kisses and acknowledge the girls as the parade passed them.

When it was time for me to go, Mom gave me the biggest hug and thanked me for everything. Although it was very difficult, the girls both signed "Thank You." This is truly one family and two little Princesses that I know I will never forget. Sincerely, Jodi

Mandy wrote: *Words fail me so I will just say* **thank you** *and pray you know how heartfelt these two words are. Know how awesome you all are and how happy you made Alex and Emma!*

She also shared that Alex recently announced that she needed to go on vacation to Cinderella's Castle.

It is with a very heavy heart that I have to inform you that Emma passed away in late March of 2012. Her father wanted us all to know how much the family appreciated everything that was done for the girls. He shared that when the girls would watch a Disney movie and see the Castle, they would say, "We've been there!" He added that Alex knows that her sister is in Heaven.

Dean visits with his Grand Marshals

MAINSTREET MEMORY 42

Jim and Shannon Shannon

Today I'd like to introduce two exceptional crew members from the Disney Cruise Line. Recognizing exceptional Guest Service has always been important to me. This chapter's title is not a typo, nor are you seeing double.

Linda and I met Shannon Bradley on one of our early Disney cruises. She was a Merchandise Manager on board the Disney Wonder. Shannon's home is Toronto, Canada. During this cruise, whenever we turned around, we ran into Shannon. We'd stroll into a shop, we'd see Shannon. We decided to pin trade one evening with the Crew...hello, Shannon. On our day at Disney's Castaway Cay, we stopped by one of the shops; you guessed it, there was Shannon! We were both impressed with this crew member's smile, attitude, and professionalism.

This young lady was a total delight, and a model crew member. We both loved seeing her, yet we needed to convince her that we were not some sort of weirdos or stalkers. As it turned out, Shannon was enjoying seeing us as well. Late in the cruise, we exchanged personal contact information.

Shannon was headed to the Magic Kingdom in just a few weeks to join her sister and her mother. She phoned that she was off the ship and would be in the Magic Kingdom the following day. We arranged to meet and I was introduced to Shannon's mother and sister. It was a very special day, as the girls were celebrating Mom's birthday. At three o'clock, the birthday girl and her two daughters led the parade as Grand Marshals.

Over the next few years, we remained in contact with Shannon. She'd come to the Orlando area on her way to or from Toronto or Port Canaveral. Our visits were frequent and our spare bedroom was designated "Shannon's room." Linda particularly enjoy these visits as the two loved shopping together. Shannon was becoming like a daughter to us.

Several visits later, Shannon shared that she was interested in a very special fellow. She had been dating him for some time and was pretty sure that he was "the one." He is a ship's officer and I remember Shannon telling me, "One day he will be Captain!" We could not wait to meet this young man, and when we did, he did not disappoint.

Jim Shannon was raised in Scarborough, England. Not long after entering college, Jim realized that this was not for him. At the age of eighteen, he boarded an oil tanker and his career at sea had begun. There are very few places in the world that Jim has not seen. He joined the Disney Cruise Line about thirteen years ago, and was recently promoted to Chief Officer of the Disney Wonder.

As it turned out, Jim was "the one" for Shannon and they have now been married for over five years. On the day of the couple's marriage at Disney's Wedding Pavilion, I escorted Shannon's grandmother down the aisle. Linda was in charge of the bride's hair and makeup, and did an amazing job...Shannon was absolutely radiant! Jim was very handsome in his tux as well.

Shannon has left the Disney Cruise Line and now manages a Disney Store in Toronto. I firmly believe that Shannon is one hundred percent correct and one day Jim will be Captain.

We do not see these two as often as we would like, yet they know that "Jim and Shannon's room" is always available for them. And yes, her married name is Shannon Shannon!

Maïnstreet Memory 43

Pomp and Circumstance

Tracy and Phil were planning the ultimate surprise for their sons, Jakob and Joshua. Phil was stationed in Iraq and was due his mid-tour leave (R and R). Jakob was about to turn twelve and would be celebrating at Walt Disney World. The plan was for Phil to "magically appear" and join the family for the big celebration. Shortly before Tracy and the boys were scheduled to head to Orlando, the Army informed Phil that he would be remaining in Iraq for several more months. All their planning had just fallen through. Although extremely disappointed, Tracy headed to WDW with the boys.

I was introduced to Tracy the day before Jakob's birthday. We talked about doing something special and agreed to meet at parade time the following day. In a way, Phil was traveling with his family. They carried a pillow with his likeness imprinted on it. The pillow would be in all the Disney photos. Tracy's parents were able to ride along to take photos and video.

Jakob and Joshua were very excited at parade time and of course, they had their special pillow with them. I'd gotten personalized Mickey Ears for the entire party, Phil included. The boys and I really connected. They declared that Disney World was their "hometown." Tracy shared that being a military child is not easy and that many feel they have no hometown, moving as often as they do. What more could a child ask for than to call Disney World home?

A few weeks later I received a letter from Tracy along with a photo of Phil. The photo was taken at Camp Slayer, Iraq...part of the Victory Base Complex. The Chief Warrant Officer Three (CW3) was dressed in his Army fatigues and was wearing his Mickey Ears. He sent a message to me that the family would be returning to Disney in about six months. Phil wanted to meet me and thank me personally for my kindness to his wife and sons.

Months later, Tracy wrote that Phil had safely returned from Iraq and provided the dates they'd be heading to Disney. The boys were excited to be heading back to their hometown. I was excited to see the boys again and could not wait to meet Phil.

Jakob and Joshua could not have been more proud to bring their Dad to their hometown. Tracy was beaming to have her family together again. Phil's handshake said thank you a thousand times. What the family did not know was that Phil was scheduled as the Honorary Veteran of the Day at the Flag Retreat Ceremony.

What I did not know was that Phil was not much of a "ceremony" kind of guy, yet he graciously accepted the invitation. After work, I met my the family and watched Phil and the Flag Retreat Ceremony. The look on the boy's faces was priceless.

After the ceremony, I said goodbye yet again to this special family. They had all been so amazing, I had truly been humbled. Tracy wrote the following regarding Flag Retreat.

Phil is not one for pomp and circumstance. He does his job and his duty to his country with pride and honor. He does not expect kudos or accolades for his service. Honoring him as the Disney World Veteran of the Day was an amazing experience. I have not seen him enjoy pomp and circumstance so much in his sixteen year military career. It was an afternoon and an honor that we will NEVER forget. Once again, THANK YOU for making our Disney dream come true!

Driving Walt's car!

MAINSTREET MEMORY 44

Mickey and Friends

Many volumes could be written about the amazing cast members at Disney. One of the most deserving is a young lady from Idaho named Megan. We worked many parades together over the years, I on the Grand Marshal side and Megan as a parade performer.

Megan began her career through Disney's College Program. She fell in love with Florida and Walt Disney World. Education was foremost for Megan and she would return to Idaho to complete her degree and graduate.

The determined young lady set three lofty goals for herself. She would return to Florida and be hired by WDW, she would work in the Entertainment Department, and she would make magic for thousands of guests.

Megan has achieved these goals and does an amazing job. Her radiant smile and positive attitude make her an outstanding cast member. She could loan the Energizer Bunny energy and her strong faith is obvious and inspirational. She is an absolute joy to be around.

Megan's path to her destination was not an easy one. One of her biggest hurdles was that her friends did not share her enthusiasm. In fact, they had a totally opposite idea of what would happen. Megan would hear comments like, "You're not good enough" and, "You'll never get hired by Disney." We were enjoying lunch together when she shared how discouraging some of her friends had become. I told Megan that I thought she did not need new dreams, but maybe she needed some new friends. Megan comes face to face with one of if not *the* most recognized figures on the planet.

Recently Megan and I had a very "Mickey" visit. It was great to catch up with my dear friend. She had been made aware of a special meet and greet. A couple was celebrating their 50th Anniversary with Mickey and Minnie. The lady, Iris, turned to them and said, "During World War II, I visited our troops in war-torn countries. When I would show anyone a photo of Mickey, their faces would light up and they would smile. You see, Mickey is very special to me...when I was a very young girl, I met Walt Disney and had my photo taken with him."

I shared my own Mickey photo story with Megan. Very early in my career with Disney at the Harmony Barber Shop, a gentleman introduced me to his daughter. She was a very pretty young lady in her late teens or early twenties. She was traveling in a wheelchair and her extreme health issues were very apparent. She was having a great day in the Magic Kingdom! I asked her father if she would enjoy a photo of Mickey. Her father replied that she would love one and gave me his mailing address. I sent the young lady an autographed eight by ten.

Many months later, Linda and I were enjoying a quiet evening at home when our phone rang. It was the young lady's father and he had "finally found me." He asked if I remembered his daughter and sending her the photo of Mickey. I answered that I did remember meeting his family. He continued that the photo had become her prized possession and was always located very near her. His daughter had endured unthinkable medical issues. On two different occasions, the doctors told the family that she would not survive the night.

The medical team often needed to try to communicate with their patient. It happened more than once that she was unable to respond...even to her own parents. Yet, she responded to the photo of Mickey with a slight squeeze of her hand. Her father added, "I just looked in on her and saw the photo of Mickey next to her and thought, I have to thank that man."

I asked Megan why she thought Mickey and Minnie have withstood the test of time and never seemed to age. Her reply was, "Simple; because they love unconditionally."

Dean along the parade route

Mainstreet Memory 45

Disney Ambassadors

Walt Disney World Ambassador, Christopher Stewart, and I teamed together to create my favorite Disney tradition. The 2004 Ambassador team of Sara, Juan, and Christopher were the first Ambassadors I hosted as Grand Marshals. I was very privileged to host every Walt Disney World Ambassador from the '04 team going forward until my retirement.

Christopher and I had become friends in the Harmony Barber Shop. He was part of Disney's College Program and loved coming to the turn of the century shop, hopefully for the great haircuts. Several years later, Christopher proposed to his beautiful wife, Michelle, in front of Cinderella's Castle. Moments after she accepted, the couple came to the barber shop to share their exciting news...I was honored.

Christopher explained that an Ambassador is a good will emissary to the world. He or she represents the spirit of the cast and the magic of Disney both internally and everywhere they visit. Their role is best described in three parts. **Cast:** To recognize and thank our Cast for their amazing efforts. **Media:** To share all the amazing offerings the WDW Resort has to share with the world. And **Community:** To "give back" to the various locations where Disney operates other than Orlando...Port Canaveral, Vero Beach etc.

Lowell Doringo, along with Michael Kelley, was an Ambassador in 2007. Lowell and I worked together to create magic for a very special couple. Several years before Lowell served as Ambassador, he was a Guest Relations Host in the Magic Kingdom. His parents were about to celebrate their thirty-fifth wedding anniversary with a trip to Hawaii. Shortly before the big day, Lowell's father required an emergency bypass operation. After his recovery, the couple headed for Disney World since the Hawaii plans were cancelled. Lowell accompanied his parents as their "exclusive" photographer as they led the parade as Grand Marshals.

Lowell and Michael later served as Ambassador Grand Marshals. After Lowell returned from a visit to see his parents, I saw him in the Magic Kingdom. Lowell rushed up and gave me a big hug. He was so excited!! He exclaimed, "Dean, My parents have the greatest fireplace mantle in the world...there are two framed Grand Marshal photos. One is of them, and one of Michael and I."

The 2009-2010 Ambassadors, Vanessa Rosas and Clay Shoemaker, were accompanied by their spouses and children during their Grand Marshal experience. I had worked with Clay as part of the Guest Relations team in the Magic Kingdom before his Ambassador role.

The 2011-2012 WDW Team of Jennifer Mason and Norman Vossschulte were joined by the Ambassadors from Disneyland Paris, Tokyo Disney, Hong Kong Disney and Disneyland California for the Grand Marshal experience. This was a "career" day for me. To host the cast members that are the very best of the best from around the world was very humbling. Their example should be imitated by each of us.

I'll close with a quote from one of the Disneyland California Ambassadors.

This experience has been very touching and incredible. We are one family and one company. We are all in it for one dream and that's creating happiness and making dreams come true.

MAiNSTREET MEMORY 46

Micah and His Mom

I've heard that there is no stronger love than that of a mother for a child. I believe my friend, Candice, will back up that statement. She was inquiring about the possibility of her son, Micah, leading a parade. The following are portions of a long letter she sent to Disney in 2006.

We have six children, four are adopted. We always knew they would all be special. One of our sons is named Micah, he is seven. We realized at age one that something was not right. This year we realized our instinct was correct. He was diagnosed with Agenisis of the Corpus Collosum. In layman's terms, he's missing tissue that connects the two halves of his brain. Chances are he will never learn past fifth or sixth grade and will always be dependent. He is a target. Other children make fun of him and pick on him because he cannot talk and articulate sounds correctly. He thinks he's stupid and knows enough to realize he's different.

Yet, we are grateful Micah is physically healthy. He does not have some horrible disease that will take him away from us. However, we have been robbed of his future. We love him with all of our hearts. I know I cannot protect him from the cruelties of other children. I cannot promise he will be able to read and spell and write like his brothers and sisters. I don't really know what I can promise him other than our love.

He loves the world and never meets a stranger. Unfortunately due to his issues he does not understand personal boundaries, so he loses friends very easily because all he wants to do is hug. I am blithering...I love him so much!

I thought I'd try in some way to show him what a very special little boy he is to the world. I do not know who this letter will reach or who may read this, but I am his mother and I will try for him. I would love for him to be in a Disney parade...any parade, any park, any day. Not even our whole family...just our special little boy. A picture we could take back and show that he was special for a moment. That nobody cared that he talked funny or looked funny. That he reads baby books in the school bus and has to take a different spelling test. That for one moment he was just "OK." I can take a picture and when things get bad for him at school, I can drag out that picture and say, "Look Micah...look how special you are." We can only wish...that is what people do when they come to Disney!

Micah, Candice, and the gang led the parade in late October. Loads of photos were taken and I lost count of the hugs given by Micah. I was on the receiving end of many of those hugs. Candice wrote in a thank you card:

Tinkerbell has nothing on you. You deserve wings because you have certainly spread some pixie dust! No amount of gratitude on my part will EVER be sufficient to repay you for the smile on his face.

He's my special boy and you have made a dream come true!

Candice shared another Story about Micah.

Funny story...We went to EPCOT for Christmas tree lighting and were rushing to get there. Micah was gawking, he gets distracted easily. We look around, and he is gone! It is packed around the tree. I'm a mess and talking with a security staff member. He asks for a description and I say he's wearing a Santa shirt and cannot talk right. Great Mother, huh?

So he gets on his radio and has umpteen staff members start looking. A few minutes later he gets a call, and they have him! It was dusk, and he was screaming and he is LOUD! At least ten mothers were trying to comfort him...not working. We meet with Micah just as they light the tree. He is screaming,"I LOVE YOU MOMMY" and there is not a dry eye within a fifty foot radius. I think we ruined at least twenty make-up jobs that night. I will go to my deathbed remembering that moment and the depth of my love for that kid. Crazy! It was just so Norman Rockwell...really very Walt Disney!

Parade step off, near Splash Mountain

MAINSTREET MEMORY 47

Bert's Big Adventure

Many of the chapters I've written feature individuals that go out of their way to create magic for others. Let me introduce you to a young couple that takes this to an entirely new level. Bert and Stacey Weiss live in Atlanta, Georgia. Bert hosts a syndicated radio show, "The Bert Show" based out of Atlanta. In 2012 the couple celebrated ten years of "Bert's Big Adventure." The following is part of their Mission Statement.

Bert's Big Adventure is a nonprofit organization that provides a magical, all expenses-paid, five-day journey to Walt Disney World for children with chronic and terminal illnesses and their families. To qualify for Bert's Big Adventure, children must be between the ages of five and twelve, live in "The Bert Show" radio listening area, prove financial need and have never been to Walt Disney World.

For several of these years, I hosted these youngsters as Grand Marshals. Bert and Stacey became my good friends in the process. Allow me to share their words about the families they bring to WDW. First, we'll hear from Bert.

The heart of Bert's Big Adventure is about connections, families connecting during stressful times, newly introduced families connecting with each other for long lasting relationships, and children connecting with other children that truly understand what it's like to live with special needs. It's about understanding the idea that, while life may be difficult, it's much easier to do it with someone else. Our entire organization is about connections.

Stacey added, *We all strive to "live in the moment." Yet for these families this is nearly impossible. The world they live in bombards them with daily challenges that most of us could not comprehend.*

For the last ten years, one hundred and ten families have had the chance to live in the moment during their five-day magical journey to Walt Disney World. For the parent it means letting go of the stress and uncertainty and crying tears of joy. For the child it means forgetting about their sickness and feeling limitless.

I'm certain each of these families would have an amazing story to share about their big adventure. The following is Noah's. The five year old was diagnosed with Down Syndrome a week after he was born. He also has an Atrioventricular Canal Defect, a congenital heart problem that occurs in only two of every ten thousand births.

Noah's mother, Tara said:

We are determined not to let his struggles define him. Instead, I see him as empowered to make a positive difference in this world. On the application for the trip, the children were asked what they want to be when they grow up. Noah's answer, "an inspiration to others." Many of Noah's most memorable experiences on the trip dealt with Mickey Mouse and seeing him in the various theme parks. While at the Saturday night dance party, the entire group watched with joy as Noah danced with

Mickey. Noah's smiles not only lit up the room but made me feel almost as if my heart would burst from my body.

Thank you, Bert and Stacey, for all that you do for Noah and his family and all the families you've touched through Bert's Big Adventure. And thank you to anyone who supports this amazing organization. You can learn more about Bert's Big Adventure at bertsbigadventure.org.

"When we know ourselves to be connected to all others, acting compassionately is simply the natural thing to do."

-Rachel Naomi Remen

Dean and his Pal, Rose

Maînstreet Memory 48

"...I Led the Disney Parade..."

Fanatic: (noun)-A person motivated by irrational enthusiasm. *"A fanatic is one who can't change his mind and won't change the subject"—Winston Churchill.* This is a fairly accurate description of Rose when it comes to the Pittsburgh Steelers. Rose does love **her** Steelers.

She also loves Walt Disney World. She loves the parks, the resorts, the cast members, and she loves the magic. I met Rose on December 5, 2002, Walt's birthday. I had selected her parents, Jim and Jenny, as Grand Marshals on their 50th wedding anniversary. Rose accompanied her parents and excitedly announced, "I led the Disney parade."

Rose and I became really close pals and would try to connect whenever she headed to WDW. I was able to surprise her and her husband, Rich, with a tour of Cinderella's Castle Suite on her birthday. Rose is a Disney Vacation Planner and does an amazing job for her clients. She loves going above and beyond for them.

Let me explain the Steeler-Disney connection. The Steelers were playing the Phoenix Cardinals in Super Bowl XLIII. Rose contacted me and asked the following, "**IF** the Steelers win the Super Bowl, will Disney honor the MVP with a parade?" Now, Rose, **IF** I had that information, you know I could not share it. Rose said she understood then said, "**When** the Steelers win the Super Bowl, will Disney honor the MVP with a parade?"

Rich and Rose decided to head to Orlando in the hopes of seeing a Steeler in the Magic Kingdom the day after the Super Bowl. Their gamble paid off! The Steelers defeated the Cardinals and MVP Santonio Holmes announced, "I'm going to Disney World!"

Monday morning, Magic Kingdom, Santonio Holmes is running very late, and it's raining. Is Rose discouraged? No, in fact she's asking where she should wait to get a good glimpse of her MVP. I suggested that she stand immediately next to the media area. Another payoff!

Rose was traveling with not only Rich, but a Mickey plush completely decked out in his Steeler uniform. A reporter from the Orlando Sentinel noticed the pint-sized Steeler and snapped a photo of Rose and Mickey on Main Street. The photo accompanied the Super Bowl feature in Tuesday's Sentinel and was also shared in Rose's local paper. Had she packed a hundred of the "Steeler" Mickeys, I'm sure she would have sold them all.

Well done, Rose. I'm positive that both Disney and the Steelers are proud to have you as one of their fanatics.

Maïnstreet Memorp 49

The Piestewa Family

<u>March 23, 2003 Nasirivyah, Iraq</u>- One wrong turn changed everything. The 507th Maintenance Company fell under attack by Iraqi insurgents just one week after the war began. Soon our nation became captivated by the story of POW Jessica Lynch. Jessica's Native American roommate and best friend, Lori Piestewa, lost her life trying to save her friend.

Piestewa was killed as she navigated her Humvee through gunfire and debris when a rocket-propelled grenade hit her truck. A member of the Hopi Tribe, Piestewa was the first woman killed in the Iraq war and believed to be the first American Indian woman killed in a foreign war.

While in Iraq, Lori told PFC Lynch that her dream was to return to the reservation in Tuba City, Arizona and build her parents a home so they could retire. Piestewa was a twenty-three-year-old divorced mother of two young children, Brandon (age 6) and Carla (age 4). The children were living in a small mobile home with Lori's parents, Percy and Terry, during her deployment.

The staff of "Extreme Makeover: Home Edition" wanted to make Lori's dream of a new home come true. The Hopi tribe had donated 1/4 acre of land for them to build upon. The family heard from well-wishers from all over the world. Her friend, PFC Lynch, was on board for the build. Neighboring tribes set aside old disputes and came together in the spirit of their warrior hero, Lori Piestewa.

During the construction the family vacationed at Walt Disney World. The families of "EMHE" are treated like royalty and much of their trip is filmed and shown during the "unveiling" of their new home. It was decided the Piestewas visit would include the Grand Marshal experience.

I hosted Lori's family in April, 2005. They could not have been more appreciative. Carla was such a doll and after parade she wanted me to hold her. When it was time to say goodbye, I was presented a photo of Lori and a copy of the Hopi Prayer. Carla whispered something to me that I did not understand. Her grandfather told me that she had just called me "uncle" in the Hopi language.

As I watched the episode of Extreme Makeover: Home Edition, I was thrilled to see this deserving family in their new home. They all had made the ultimate sacrifice. Jessica Lynch said it best: "We were not similar in size, frame, race, religion, or origin, but in our friendship, only one heart existed with two people connected."

Mainstreet Memory 50

My Window on Main Street

Do you think people are *really* listening when you are speaking? Do they *really* hear what you say? Here's a letter from a guest who was listening...*very* closely.

Dean, On one of my many visits to the Magic Kingdom (specifically, January 24, 2006), we met to say hello. You mentioned that you had something for us, and arranged to meet us later. When we met I recognized the book you were carrying. It was the special Cast Member book for the celebration of the 50th Anniversary of Disneyland named "The Magic Begins With Me."

You proceeded to tell your story as to how you got selected for this book. You let me read the section dedicated to you. It was so touching. It made me realize what a great job you had with Disney and you are definitely an asset being in this position.

Dean, you started your story by saying,"Since I will probably never have a window on Main Street, this is the next best thing." You are such a good storyteller that by the time you finished, I was in tears. With this story in the Cast Member book you have made a huge contribution to the history of Walt Disney World,

I have all kinds of books on Disney history and now I knew I wanted this book for my library, especially since I knew you were in this book. This is when you surprised Jerry and I by presenting us with our signed copy. I was overwhelmed with happiness. You made our many visits to WDW so Magical and this was the icing on the cake with a cherry on top. Each visit you greeted us with a smile on your face.

Over the years, you and I would discuss retirement, not knowing when it would happen for either of us. Since I recently retired I knew that I needed to do something special for your retirement. Your comment about a window on Main Street stuck with me.

With the window in mind I took tons of photos along Main Street. Since you started as a barber, the Harmony Barber Shop looked better and better for what I wanted to do. The barber shop window now has your name with your title as the Grand Marshal Coordinator in your shadow box. Dean, you will always have a window on Main Street to us! Thank You for giving us a Magical Memory every time we saw you at The Magic Kingdom. Lots of love and hugs, Carol and Jerry

For those of you not familiar with the windows on Main Street, these windows are dedicated to people that have a special connection to Disney. Each window has a pseudo business name. An example is my friend, Lee Cockerell's window. His window reads: The Main Street Diary, True Tales of Inspiration, Lee A. Cockerell, Editor-In-Chief. Lee is retired Executive Vice President of WDW Operations.

Thank you, Carol and Jerry, for this beautiful and unique gift. I appreciate all the time and effort that went into its creation. Thank you for your kind words and kind thoughts. And thank you, Carol, for being such a good listener.

Terry Gaschler celebrating with his brother as
Grand Marshal, June 14, 2012, Dean's last
official day as a Disney Cast Member

MAiNSTREET MEMORY 51

The King and I

Not many personalities are as easy to recognize as Richard Petty. His signature cowboy hat and wrap-around sunglasses accompanied by that amazing smile are hard to miss. His success as a race car driver earned him the nickname *"King Richard"* or simply *"The King."*

Arrangements had been made for Petty, his wife, and several of their grandchildren to celebrate his birthday as Grand Marshals. This was all happening around the July 4th weekend. Each year a major NASCAR race happens in Daytona around this holiday.

The King was a great sport and eager to participate in the parade festivities, placing a set of Mickey ears atop his cowboy hat. It was very evident the couple adored their grandkids. The family boarded the Main Street Fire Engine, with Richard seated next to the driver...no way were we going to let him drive!

What the Pettys did not know was that we'd arranged a little surprise for our birthday boy. As we left Frontierland, The Dapper Dans were busy on Main Street. The guys were informing the guests about King Richard's big day. The vehicle came to a stop on Main Street and the quartet escorted Petty to the center of the street. Then the Dans yelled to the crowd, "All right, one, two, three!" Several hundred guests then sang "Happy Birthday." As Petty returned to join his family, the crowd was cheering wildly. He thanked and re-thanked them. We had caught The King completely off guard; he was truly humbled.

Richard was scheduled for a meeting after the parade and Mrs. Petty and the kids were anxious to play in the Magic Kingdom. As I escorted The King backstage, we had just one small problem: no ride. His driver was running late. Suddenly, I had about fifteen minutes, one-on-one, with a racing legend.

What were we going to talk about to kill some time? How about cars, how about race cars? During this time, Petty spoke about changes over the years in the sport of racing, driver safety, and the fans. Never did he mention his own accomplishments or how he became "The King."

Before we knew it, we were saying goodbye. Richard could not thank me enough for all the wonderful things that had happened with his wife and grandkids. We shook hands and away he went. I do not know a great deal about auto racing. I do know that I met a true gentleman the day I met Richard Petty.

Mainstreet Memory 52

Garrison's Perfect Letter

In August of 2003, I received the following letter. It was from a young man named Garrison who was 9 years old.

Dear Grand Marshal Picker, My Mom is a Disney maniac. My Mom wants to go to Disney every year. Her name is Lori and she just turned 40. The trip is her birthday gift. We are going Dec. 5-13. I have a one year old brother named Sammy. Everybody asks if she is his grandma. It makes her very sad. My sister Grace is 7. Please let my Mom be in a parade. I'll give you $5.00. It could make her happy again. Thanks, Garrison

The following letter from Lori accompanied Garrison's.

Dear Guest Relations, I am aware that Grand Marshals for parades are not selected this way. I certainly understand why. Garrison is 9 years old. He is severely dyslexic with learning disabilities across the board. He attends a private school for learning disabilities. His homework this summer was to continue reading and writing. His teacher (who also loves Disney) gave him the idea to write to Disney.

Garrison worked on this letter off and on all summer. He said, "It has to be perfect with no mistakes." I know that I have a wonderful son. He faces many challenges on a daily basis. He tries very hard and makes straight A's. I'm sure from this letter you can tell he has a heart of gold. I'm already planting seeds in his mind about Disney's College Program. **I can dream, can't I!** *Have a magical day. Sincerely, Lori*

When I responded to Garrison, I thanked him for his *perfect letter!* I explained that I could not promise or guarantee that Lori would be in a parade, and that I would try very hard to help make her trip to Disney special. I signed it...Dean, The Grand Marshal Picker.

In December, Garrison's dream came true as his Mom, Lori, (the Disney maniac) and her family led a Disney parade! I'll share part of Lori's thank you note.

Thank you for what you did for our family and Garrison last December. Garrison was so proud to have made his parents so happy. Grace just slipped her hand into yours and would have gone anywhere with you. You see, the Walt Disney World Resort is the one place in the world where our son doesn't have any worries, and he is treated just like everybody else. We forget about all of the hardships and struggles that we have in our lives. Dean, thank you for the great warmth and kindness you showed our family. We love you! Yours truly, Lori

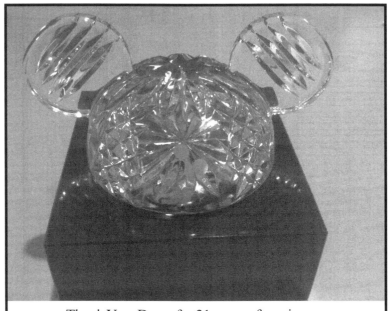

Thank You, Dean, for 21 years of service.

Maïnstreet Memory 53

Youthful Exuberance

...it was like something good was stuck in my heart and I never wanted it to come out...

Earlier in this book I defined exuberance as joyful enthusiasm. Kelly is another prime example of that definition. I met Kelly and her family in 2005, she was thirteen at the time. After participating as Grand Marshal, Kelly shared the following.

Dear Dean, Thank you so much for giving me the most magical day of my life! I had the greatest day ever. Gees, now I know what movie stars feel like. It has always been a dream of mine to be in the Disney parade. While watching the parade one day I remember whispering to my mom, 'maybe that will be us some day.' Boy, little did I know. When I first met you, I had no idea the magic you'd bring.

When you asked if we wanted to be in the parade, at first I couldn't breathe. I wanted to say yes, but I was too excited to talk. Then as I was jumping for joy hysterically, I'm like yes, oh my gosh, it's a dream come true! I was thinking, wow, I'll be part of Disney history and I'll be riding in a car smiling for millions and billions of people and not know any of them. Wow, I'm getting goose bumps now just thinking of the magic.

I could hardly wait all day. I was thinking wow I'm going to be in the parade. When we headed for Frontierland, I'm dancing for joy all the way there. The excitement got bigger and bigger. I'm nearly in tears thinking wow it's a magical miracle that this happened to us.

But then you told us that the car we would be riding in was one Walt Disney rode in. The man I've done six biographies on and wasn't allowed to do one on him this year, my idol, and hereby the man with the greatest dream ever, out came the tears.

You were right about being in photo albums across America, I've never gotten my picture taken by so many people. It was amazing smiling and waving and just feeling the magic. What is almost impossible to describe is that magic feeling I got, it was like something good was stuck in my heart and I never wanted it to come out!

We have our parade picture (which is sitting in our cabinet for everyone to see), but even if we didn't, I would remember this for infinity and beyond! Thank you again for the most magical day of my life. And may all your days be magical! Love Kelly, Future Cast Member

I'm going to go out on a limb and suggest that this young lady loves anything remotely related to Disney. Would you agree? A little follow-up...as a freshman Kelly applied for Disney's College Program and was accepted. Kelly moved from her home in Buffalo, New York to Orlando to be part of Disney. Her childhood dream to become a Disney Cast Member is a reality.

Kelly continued her education while working part-time for Disney. Shortly after graduating, she was offered a full-time position. Now Kelly is the one responsible for "something good" stuck in the hearts of Disney Guests.

I am so proud of her.

Concluding this book on a positive and upbeat note was most important to me. With young and amazing talent like Kelly that is commonplace at Walt Disney World, the Company will remain Number One in family entertainment for decades to come.

Thank you for taking time to read about the incredible individuals I was so fortunate to come in contact with during my time with Disney. The reality is that I was the one that was blessed to meet them. I came away with something good stuck in my heart and I never want it to come out.

ABOUT THE AUTHOR

"A memoir allows you to connect on a personal level with complete strangers"

A brief history: Originally from Kansas, I settled in Florida via Colorado. I was hired by the Walt Disney Company (Walt Disney World / Magic Kingdom Park) in 1991. It all began in The Harmony Barber Shop, just off Main Street USA. Seven years later, I assumed the role of Grand Marshal Coordinator for the daily Parade in The Magic Kingdom. The remaining fourteen years were spent creating and sharing magic with the nearly 7,000 families I'd selected for Parade Grand Marshals. I retired on June 14, 2012.

As a kid who grew up on a farm in Kansas, I used to watch *"Disney's Wonderful World of Color"* every Sunday night. My hope was that one day I'd be able to visit Disneyland in California. I never thought the direction of my life would allow not only seeing Disney's Parks but fulfilling the dreams of many Disney Guests. And my wildest dream would not have included a personal Disney Story to share. So, if you are reading this, my own hopes and dreams have come true!

Some of my experiences as Grand Marshal Coordinator may make you laugh, while others may make you reach for a tissue. My intent is to share my unique perspective of the afternoon parade. Many friends and family members have been telling me for years that I should share these amazing stories. Me? Write a book? The longer I thought about it, the more sense it began to make. After all, wasn't Walt Disney a storyteller? I believe I'm in pretty good company.

During my career I've hosted Super Bowl MVP's, World Series Champions, Olympic Gold Medalists, Heavyweight Boxing Champions, Indy and NASCAR Racing Champions, Astronauts, Miss America(s), TV & Motion Picture Actors, and Recording Artists as Parade Grand Marshals. However, these celebrated figures are not the focus of this book.

The real focal points are the families that came through the gates of The Magic Kingdom on a daily basis. In many of these true life stories you will see individuals that have the heart of a champion. I'm humbled and proud to share these amazing stories.

I've heard it said, *"Find a job you love and you will never work a day in your life."* I was truly blessed to have a job that I loved. A dear friend told me, "Dean, what you have here are *emotional slices of life."* Please enjoy.